SAMLA STUDIES IN MILTON

SAMLA STUDIES IN MILTON

Essays on
John Milton and His Works

BY

Members of the South Atlantic Modern Language Association

EDITED BY

J. MAX PATRICK
Queens College of the City of New York

FOREWORD BY

JAMES HOLLY HANFORD
Professor Emeritus, Western Reserve University

UNIVERSITY OF FLORIDA PRESS
GAINESVILLE

1953

A University of Florida Press Book

JAMES HOLLY HANFORD

Foreword

THE LIFE AND WORKS of the poet Milton may seem to some persons a subject sufficiently remote from current interest and the continued publication of books about him an illustration of the mere *vis inertiae* of scholarly tradition. His life was written in considerable detail four times in the quarter century after his death, and the process of preparing learned editions, beginning with that of Patrick Hume in 1695, had already reached the point of a six-volume variorum by 1801. When David Masson finished his monumental work in 1894, it might fairly have been thought that the account was nearly closed. No other English author, not Shakespeare himself, had been the occasion of so vast an accumulation of fact and of opinion. Actually, the concern of the critical and learned world with Milton did fall off, but only for a time. Its revival was something bound to occur, if only because scholars soon discovered that the barrel of ascertainable information was by no means empty. Almost every page of Masson, almost every note of Todd, invited amplification if not revision. There were important documents which not even they had taken account of or even seen. Milton's own great learning, the variety of his achievement, and his long involvement with public events and political controversy left open trails which proved hardly less rewarding than those which had already been explored.

That the invitation thus afforded has been picked up most vigorously in America is due to a variety of causes, most

obvious among them being the general stimulation afforded
by the development of higher education, with its concomi-
tant emphasis on humanistic research in graduate schools
as a preparation for college teaching. In the early phases of
the exploitation of English literature—the most popular field
of advanced study—Chaucer and Shakespeare were the great
figures. Milton was perhaps a natural third, both in point of
chronology and in intrinsic interest from the scholar's stand-
point. If he seemed at first not to need elucidation, neither
had they before the methods of modern philological and
historical inquiry did their work. Once in the current of
research, Milton proved fruitful and exciting enough and
the volume of publication regarding him has come almost
to equal the output of Shakespeare studies, which have a
way of flowing perennially, whether school keeps or not.

There are, however, better reasons for the continuance
of Milton study than the fact that there is plenty left to
know about him. He stands as one of the heroes of the
race, as an immense symbolic figure about whom men will
be curious and feel strongly as long as there is any sort of
remembrance of things past among them. For Americans
he is of all English writers the most nearly like a founding
father. His ethical and religious idealism came over with
the New England Puritans, as he might have come himself.
He stood for liberalism and the separation of the Church
and State. He helped formulate the principles of government and he implemented the cause of freedom. More than
that, he was one of the Springs of Helicon of which every
schoolboy had at least the opportunity to drink. And finally,
having taken sides on fundamental issues (philosophical,
religious, and aesthetic) which permanently divide mankind,
he remained controversial in terms of the living present.

It is not possible for such a figure to be forgotten but it is
possible for him to become a stereotype in popular opinion,
and the formulae with which he seems to be settled in one

generation may persist even in the most authoritative writing of later times. These formulae may be wrong or misleading. Anyone, of course, can test them by a new inspection of the object itself, but to do so successfully is an expert task, involving much more than knowledge of the obvious and immediate data. In Milton's case, it involves a whole background of literature and history and the collaborative activity of many minds, working often in small compartments and bringing to the task a great variety of special skills.

The present volume is a fair sampling of modern Milton scholarship. The studies are necessarily limited in scope but their broader bearings are suggested. It is one of the characteristics of Milton study that it quickens interest in many fields. Though they are related to each other only in the sense that they all deal directly with Milton instead of using Milton as a starting point for some larger subject, certain connections among them are apparent.

The first and second, "Milton's Views on Universal and Civil Decay" and "The Substance of Milton's Angels," deal with key concepts in his political and metaphysical philosophy. They belong in general to the history of ideas but they illuminate also his individual attitude and clarify his objectives both as a teacher and an artist. The problem of progress or decline in human affairs and the problem of the nature of the spiritual world are perennial. Milton's reactions to them, operating in the milieu of formulations current in his time, were complex. The analyses in these articles not only enable us to measure the difference between his world and ours, but bring us into a closer relation to his emotional and imaginative experience. They enable us also to read his prose and poetry with a sharper sense of its finer meanings and a more balanced understanding of the whole.

The other studies concern themselves with various aspects of his style and language and, by extension, with the spirit and temper, as contrasted with the ideological content, of his work. The subject of Milton's vocabulary, treated in the essay by Professor Boone, is an old one. Her minute examination of Book VI of *Paradise Lost* is a step toward a definitive answer to the question of what kind of English Milton uses and what he actually has contributed to the language. Professor Thaler's paper adds a new body of evidence to the case for Milton's intimate knowledge of the plays of Shakespeare and of his dependence on him for poetic imagery and phrase. It is hard to believe that future research will reveal many more parallels than Thaler has accumulated in this and his earlier articles on the subject. Of somewhat different character is the contribution to poetic origins in "*Lycidas* and the Marinell Story." Spenser was perhaps Milton's greatest source of imaginative inspiration among his English predecessors, and much has been written of their relationship. Professor Stroup proposes a new episode in the *Faerie Queene* as having integrated itself with other suggestions in Milton's mind and furnished a vital element in the idea and imagery of *Lycidas*. The discovery commends itself and enhances our sense of the richness of the tradition which embodies itself in this poem. While doing nothing to detract from Milton's originality, since the transformation into a new substance is complete, it further defines the essential character of an art which deliberately nourishes itself out of the beauty of the past.

To see the object as in itself it really is, is the common goal of critical and factual scholarship, and freshness of approach is often as important as new information in attaining it. "The Accent on Youth in *Comus*" senses a quality in this production which has been obscured in recent discussion. Milton wrote for the young and the masque speaks their natural language, the more successfully because he himself was young. In this view, *Comus* is not subject to the impatient or even hostile treatment which has been accorded it by some critics—Swinburne, for example, who described it as the "faultless but scentless reproduction of a rose in academic wax for the admiration of such craftsmen as must confine their ambitions to the laurels of a college or the plaudits of a school." There is a relationship, somewhat paradoxical to be sure, between this study and Professor Gilbert's discussion of Milton's defense of bawdry. The latter article strikes a lively note in the solemn halls of Milton scholarship. In finding the comedy of sex in certain passages in *Paradise Lost*, Gilbert further modifies the Puritan stereotype, and does something to integrate elements in Milton's character as a writer which have seemed to be in violent contradiction.

It is apparent that the issues in these last articles are not issues of historical fact, though historical fact has a bearing on them. The aim of the Professor Ants Oras' concluding study, on the other hand, is to determine a point in literary biography for which the data have hitherto been inconclusive. It is an impressive illustration of the application of scientific method to a problem in which the observed phenomena are a poet's practices in the use of his aesthetic medium. Such a method was long ago applied to the plays of Shakespeare, though never, to my knowledge, so ingeniously or with such a variety of complementary approaches. The results will be appraised by a few specialists and the conclusions incorporated in the total structure of knowledge of and about Milton. It would be the merest stultification to deprecate the expense of human resources which goes into such an investigation. The chronology of Milton's poetry is basic to any account of his development and therefore to our understanding of his personality and of the workings of his imagination.

There are, moreover, in the case of this as of the other studies in the present volume, incidental results which may be valuable independently of the specific conclusions aimed at. Milton himself fully recognized the claims of truth to the allegiance of the human mind and thought no effort wasted in pursuing it. He deplored mere roving speculation but his own instincts were exploratory and in his finest utterances on this subject he is more conscious of the fruitfulness than of the dangers of free questing after the unknown. "To be still searching what we know by what we know not, still closing up truth to truth as we find it, this is the golden rule in theology as well as in arithmetic." It is the golden rule also in the study of the humanities to which the contributors of this volume are committed.

To conclude these preliminary remarks I would like to call attention to the regional character of the present publication as something not wholly accidental or without significance. The commonwealth of learning transcends the boundaries of time or place and that is its chief glory. But scholarship cannot thrive in isolation and it has always been animated by communal loyalties. The great achievements of Milton's own epoch were at once national and international and he himself was one in whom local patriotism cohered with citizenship in the universal community of civilized mankind. American scholars in literature have always been in friendly competition with those of other countries, particularly England. That we are late comers and, as it were, intruders into a field already so well cultivated by its first possessors perhaps explains our zeal. It would be a blessing to the world if these were the dominant rivalries among individuals, groups, and nations, for, as Dante beautifully says of the enjoyment of spiritual as opposed to material goods:

> *Per quanti si dice più il "nostro,"*
> *Tanto possiede più di ben ciascuno,*
> *E più di caritate arde in quel chiostro.*

J. Max Patrick

Editor's Introduction

THIS VOLUME is a regional product prepared by members of the South Atlantic Modern Language Association to advance the world-wide appreciation of Milton's works and to make better known the scholarly achievements of the universities of the southeastern United States. The remarkable efflorescence of education in that area during the twentieth century, particularly during the past twenty-five years, bears fruit in such a collection as this one. But to call this movement a product of a "cultural Renaissance" in the South would be false, for it represents a continuation of the long-established academic tradition of such States as Virginia and North Carolina, in combination with a pioneer growth of the highest levels of education in such a state as Florida.

The principle of regionalism as a prime basis for these studies may be justified from parallels in the works of Milton himself. In Scripture he discovered that God particularly favored the land of Canaan, and in history, that heaven was "in a peculiar manner propitious and propending" toward the realm of England. Milton thus recognized the fact that particular regions and peoples sometimes make distinctive advances. He not only chose to write his major poems in what in the seventeenth century was a regional language— English—but also wrote histories of such special areas as Britain and Muscovy. In short, he was himself a regionalist; and as such, he would have acknowledged the validity of an anthology representative of South Atlantic scholarship.

Milton was, of course, both less than a regionalist and more than one: he was an individual and a humanist, as well as an Englishman. Similarly, the present volume has been composed by individuals, each pursuing special scholarly interests; but they write not merely as individuals, or as Southerners, but also as universal scholars in the international community of learned men. Some of them are Southerners by birth and training; others, by adoption, choice, or accident. Their backgrounds range from the universities of the northern United States to those of England and Estonia.

The preparation of the volume has been in many ways a model of cooperative scholarship. The project was initiated by the Spenser-Milton discussion group at one of the annual conventions of the South Atlantic Modern Language Association. The following procedure was adopted. Scholars in the southeastern United States were invited to contribute articles. These were submitted to the editor and then passed on to other Miltonists in the area for evaluations, comments, and suggestions. The criticisms made were both helpful and unrestrained: they revealed vast resources of scholarly competence and vitality. As a result, a number of contributions were withdrawn. Those that remained were submitted to further scrutiny by other Milton specialists in the region. In most cases their appraisals led to extensive revisions of the original manuscripts. No article was accepted for publication without the approval of scholars in at least three universities in the area. When disputes as to the merits of a contribution arose, as many as twelve professors in as many universities and colleges were called upon for their criticisms and evaluations. The final choice was thus a cooperative one, and, in some measure, so are the final products. But inclusion of an article does not necessarily imply that it was approved by all members of the board of consultants: Only one article in the present volume met with the unanimous approval of Miltonists in the three universities to which it was sent.

Many of the consultants read and passed judgment upon only one or two of the articles. Accordingly, the responsibility for each study rests solidly in its author, although the ultimate responsibility for each inclusion lies with the editor acting primarily on a basis of evaluations presented by at least three Miltonists in different institutions in the southeastern area, and only secondarily on his own opinion of the work in question. The editor's role has been chiefly that of liaison officer, as one of many critics of the works submitted, and as an agent for seeing the complete collection through the press.

ACKNOWLEDGMENTS

The Editor gratefully acknowledges the expert assistance of the following scholars as Editorial Consultants in the preparation of this volume:

Robert H. West (Georgia), Thomas B. Stroup (Kentucky), Ants Oras (Florida), Arthur D. Matthews (Miami), George P. Hayes (Agnes Scott), John L. Lievsay (Tennessee), Alwin Thaler (Tennessee), Robert H. Bowers (Florida), Milledge B. Siegler (South Carolina), Kester Svendsen (Oklahoma), Arthur K. Moore (Kentucky), C. E. Mounts (Florida), William B. Hunter, Jr. (Wofford), Alton C. Morris (Florida), Thomas Pyles (Florida), Lalia Phipps Boone (Florida), Allan H. Gilbert (Duke), and B. Q. Morgan (Stanford).

Special thanks are due to Robert H. West and Thomas B. Stroup, who submitted detailed and very helpful comments on a number of the studies. Indeed, Dr. West's assessments were so considerable and so useful that he could almost be listed as a joint editor, were it not for the fact that he had no connection with the final revisions of the manuscript and the actual publication of this collection.

Contents

JOSEPH ALLEN BRYANT, JR.

Milton's Views on
Universal and Civil Decay

THE POSITION OF JOHN MILTON in the seventeenth-century controversy about universal decay has until recently received almost no attention.[1] Most commentators have been content to observe merely that his youthful opinions on the subject, as reflected in the little poem *Naturam non pati senium* (1628), seem to place him well within the ranks of those "optimists" who denied that the world is subject to decay.[2] To this evidence we can add, for whatever it may be worth, a passage near the end of the *Seventh Prolusion* in which Milton represented a desperate and dying Ignorance as using "the decadent old age of the world" and the approaching "speedy destruction of all things" to argue the futility of all man's efforts and aspirations.[3] Milton's answer to Ignorance here indicates that he shared the popular belief in the imminence of the end of the world, but it still leaves us ample room to doubt whether

---

1. For a general discussion of this controversy, see R. F. Jones, *Ancients and Moderns: A Study of the Background of the "Battle of the Books"* (St. Louis, 1936), pp. 23-42; and Ernest Lee Tuveson, *Millennium and Utopia: A Study in the Background of the Idea of Progress* (Berkeley, Calif., 1949), pp. 22-74.
2. The term "optimists" in this application stems from E. M. W. Tillyard, *The Elizabethan World Picture* (New York, 1944), p. 33.
3. See *The Works of John Milton*, ed. F. A. Patterson *et al.* (New York, 1931-1938), XII, 279. Subsequent references to Milton's works are to this, the Columbia edition.

1

he was willing to accept the popular view of a decadent world.

In any case, Milton's college exercises do not necessarily give us his private convictions; and, even if they do, they by no means preclude the possibility that he later changed his mind. In fact, several passages in the English prose works suggest that, in spite of what he had said as a youth, Milton did come to fear inwardly what Donne once described as "a sensible decay and age in the whole frame of the world, and every piece thereof."[4] In this connection, Professor Zera S. Fink[5] calls our attention to the frequency of the word "degenerate" in *The Tenure of Kings and Magistrates*[6] and in the *Ready and Easy Way*,[7] to Milton's references to the "fate of the age" in *The Reason of Church Government*[8] and in *Paradise Lost*,[9] and to the whole of his admonition of Parliament in *Areopagitica*.[10] These passages, Professor Fink believes, show that Milton at some time or other before 1642 came to accept, if only subconsciously, the deteriorist theory which as a student he had ridiculed, and that he was not altogether able to keep it from influencing his mature thinking.

On the surface, this conclusion appears reasonable enough. Since the passages cited do indicate clearly that Milton was troubled by a fear of some kind of decay when he wrote them, it is quite natural to suppose that the cause of his concern was that specter of universal decay which had been troubling the souls of so many devout Protestants during

4. Sermon XXXVI.
5. *The Classical Republicans: An Essay in the Recovery of a Pattern of Thought in Seventeenth Century England*, Northwestern University Studies in the Humanities, No. 9 (Evanston, Ill., 1945), p. 91.
6. *Works*, V, 41.
7. *Works*, VI, 117.
8. *Works*, III, 237.
9. *Works*, II, 261-262.
10. *Works*, IV, 344 ff.

the preceding half a century. Now, the purpose of this study is to offer another, and I believe more satisfactory, way of looking at those passages; but it must be admitted that one of them does seem to refer to universal decay. In *Paradise Lost* Milton says specifically:

> . . . *unless an age too late, or cold*
> *Climat, or Years damp my intended wing*
> *Deprest*. . . .[11]

Even this, however, does not give us any conclusive proof that Milton personally feared "an age too late"; for, as Professor Fink himself has suggested,[12] Milton's probable purpose in these lines was to emphasize the idea of divine inspiration. The mention of three facts prejudicial to his art is to be taken not as a reference to specific personal fears, but simply as a rhetorical device.

The other passages which have been cited are very likely serious expressions of Milton's mature views; but they need to be read primarily, I think, as evidence of Milton's political theory rather than as evidence of his suppressed opinions about the stability or instability of the visible universe. As I shall attempt to show, it was Milton's political theory, not his cosmology, that caused him occasionally to reflect soberly and perhaps fearfully on such subjects as degeneration, decay, and the fate of the age. Nevertheless, political theory and cosmology, at least in Milton's case, are related. Milton's concept of the universe reinforced and gave meaning to his concept of the state; for this reason, if for no other, we need to examine first his opinion about the nature of the universe and decide with as much finality as the evidence will permit whether or not he thought it subject to decay.

11. *PL* IX.44-46.
12. "Milton and the Theory of Climatic Influence," *MLQ*, II (1941), 67-80.

I

As far as the deteriorist theory itself is concerned, there are almost no specific references in Milton's works to support any conclusion, one way or the other. If we disregard those passages which have been cited as references to it (and as such I believe we must disregard them), we have left only the discussion in *Naturam non pati senium*. This, though positive enough in its statements against the theory, can also be disregarded, as being only a piece of *juvenilia* and at best a risky guide to the poet's mature opinions. Yet we really do not need specific references to the deteriorist theory to be reasonably certain that Milton believed in a stable universe.

In the first place, all the pertinent passages in Milton's *Christian Doctrine* suggest a universe that is essentially stable. From that work we learn that in the beginning God made the visible world, as he made all creation, through the agency of the Son,[13] and that the Son has ever since upheld, or preserved, all things "by the word of his [that is, God's] power."[14] The means whereby the Son has preserved this creation, however, is God's providence, and providence consists of an "immutable order of causes appointed by him in the beginning."[15] Now, providence, Milton says, is commonly, and indeed too frequently, referred to as "nature": "for nature cannot possibly mean anything but the mysterious power and efficacy of that divine voice which went forth in the beginning, and to which, as to a perpetual command, all things have since paid obedience."[16] This does not mean that the universe has remained just as it was when God created it. Milton is careful to explain that God preserves

13. *Works*, XIV, 323.
14. *Works*, XIV, 325.
15. *Works*, XV, 93.
16. *Ibid.*

the world only so far as regards its existence and not as regards its primitive perfection.[17] After the fall of man, sin and death entered into the world; and all creatures, once preserved absolutely, became subject to mutability, the mark of Satan and of sin.[18] Yet we are not to infer from this that the substance of the world thereby became degenerate. "Matter, . . ." Milton explains, "proceeded incorruptible from God; and even since the fall it remains incorruptible as far as concerns its essence."[19] Thus, according to *Christian Doctrine*, matter must remain incorruptible until God receives it back into Himself, and nature must remain a "mysterious power and efficacy" until God's decrees shall have been fulfilled in that final conflagration at the end of time.

All this accords very well with what we learn about the state of the universe from Milton's *Paradise Lost*. Significantly, in all the long description of the changes that occurred in the universe after Adam's disobedience there is no mention of universal decay.[20] Nor is there so much as a hint of it in Michael's long survey of world history. There is ample recognition of the "sway of Mutability," to be sure, and of the spiritual perversion that Satan will effect before he is finally subdued, but there is no suggestion of a progressive and consistent decline, physical or spiritual. Milton's conclusion is simply

> *so shall the World goe on,*
> *To good malignant, to bad men benigne,*
> *Under her own waight groaning, till the day*
> *Appeer of respiration to the just,*
> *And vengeance to the wicked. . . .*[21]

17. *Works*, XV, 59.
18. *Works*, XV, 25.
19. *Works*, XV, 23-25.
20. *PL* X.651 ff.
21. *PL* XII.537-541.

Actually, there is nothing in either *Christian Doctrine* or *Paradise Lost*—or, for that matter, in any other work by Milton—which precludes our regarding the description of the universe in *Naturam non pati senium* as an accurate and adequate statement of Milton's mature opinion; and for that reason we can hardly afford to ignore it entirely. Readers will recall that the poem begins with a stricture upon those who would presumptuously impute their own imperfect concept of things to the eternal gods.[22] This is followed by some sixty-two lines in which Milton asserts his faith that the same heavenly bodies will continue always to follow their accustomed courses through the same zodiac, and that year after year the winds will still blow as vigorously as ever, the sea replenish perennially its supply of sportive whales, and the earth bring forth in appropriate season similar blooms of undiminished sweetness. In this way, he concludes, all things must necessarily go on, forever changing yet never declining, until the hour of that final conflagration which God has decreed from the beginning.

The description which Milton gives us here has nothing new in it. In fact, in outline it is so remarkably similar to the one in George Hakewill's lengthy *Apologie or Declaration of the Power and Providence of God in the Government of the World* (1627) that scholars have frequently suggested the possibility of Milton's being indebted to Hakewill. A quotation from Hakewill's own summary will serve to illustrate:

Although the CREATOUR and Disposer of all things hath left all Particulars and Individualls, under the circle of the Moone, to the stroake of Tyme and Death; yet by His powerfull Hand He holdeth backe the Sythe of Tyme from destroying or impayring the Universe: Though the same Hand shall at last destroy the Whole by Fire. . . . So though

---

22. For the text of the poem see *Works*, I, 260-264.

there be many changes and variations in the World, yet all things come about one time or another to the same points againe. And there is nothing new under the Sunne.[23]

But, striking as the correspondence between these two statements is, it really gives us no definite answer to the question of Milton's indebtedness to Hakewill. The reason for this is that the concept of universal order expressed by both writers is a commonplace of ancient standing. It is at least as old as Plato's *Timaeus,* which, thanks to Cicero's translation, influenced not only Renaissance thought but medieval as well. Christian writers, both Catholic and Protestant, had made extensive use of the concept, and Milton undoubtedly knew several versions of it.[24] Indeed, he had only to turn to Spenser's *Mutabilitie Cantos* to find an excellent exposition by that Protestant poet whom he later called "a better teacher than Aquinas." Spenser's verdict, as delivered by the goddess Nature, is as follows:

> *I well consider all that ye haue sayd,*
>> *And find that all things stedfastnes doe hate*
>> *And changed be: yet being rightly wayd*
>> *They are not changed from their first estate;*
>> *But by their change their being doe dilate:*
>> *And turning to themselues at length againe,*
>> *Doe worke their owne perfection so by fate:*
>> *Then ouer them Change doth not rule and raigne;*
> *But they raigne ouer change, and doe their*
>> *states maintaine.*[25]

23. Hakewill placed this statement on the page facing the illustrated title page of his second edition (1630) with the caption "The Argument of the Front and of the Worke."

24. A comparison of Milton's *Seventh Prolusion (Works,* XII, 253-257) with the *Timaeus* (89E-90D) will suggest that the versions with which Milton was familiar may have included Plato's. There are good brief discussions of some of the more widely known statements of this concept in Tillyard, pp. 7-33.

25. *FQ* VII.vii.58.

To put it briefly, Milton, in professing to believe in cyclic change rather than in progressive decay, was simply taking the position that we should normally expect a Christian humanist to take. His works show that this was the position consistent with his theology and the one he was prepared publicly to acknowledge. It can also be shown, I think, that he maintained this position without the occasional misgivings that seem to be indicated by his references to the imminence of decay; but that task requires us to turn from the broad picture of the universe and examine in detail Milton's view of a particular kind of sublunar cycle—that of a body politic.

II

In general, it can be said that Milton's references to decay derive their significance from his assumption that bodies politic, like the human beings who compose them, have distinct sublunar identities in their own right and are therefore, like all other creatures under the moon, subject to change and decay. The principal repository for his views on this subject is his first prelatical pamphlet, *Of Reformation,* written and published in 1641. In that work, near the beginning of the second book, we find him drawing upon the classic analogy between the commonwealth and a human body:

. . . a Commonwelth ought to be but as one huge Christian personage, one mighty growth, and stature of an honest man, as big, and compact in vertue as in body; for looke what the grounds, and causes are of a single happines to one man, the same yee shall find them to a whole state, as *Aristotle* both in his ethicks, and politiks, from the principles of reason layes down. . . .[26]

26. *Works,* III, 38. The references to Aristotle are to *Politics* VII.i ff., and *Nichomachean Ethics* I.ii.

Farther on in the same treatise Milton returned to this analogy to explain the basic principle of the mixed constitution:

And because things simply pure are inconsistent in the
masse of nature, nor are the elements or humors in Mans
Body exactly *homogeneall,* and hence the best founded Com-
mon-wealths, and least barbarous have aym'd at a certaine
mixture and temperament, partaking the severall vertues of
each other State, that each part drawing to it selfe may keep
up a steddy, and eev'n uprightness in common.[27]

This passage, of course, gives us pretty clear evidence of
Milton's sympathy with the views of those classical republicans of the day who were advocating a Polybian mixed
constitution for England;[28] but it shows also that he took the
commonplace analogy between a state and the human body
seriously enough to draw conclusions from it. Clearly, in
Milton's opinion, the body politic and the body of man are
both partakers of the "masse of nature" and both are subject
to her laws.

The strength of this analogy in Milton's thinking is indicated by still another passage in *Of Reformation.* In this one
he showed, by an approving reference to Polybius, that he
was familiar with much of the republicanism of his own day:

There is no Civill *Government* that hath beene known, no
not the *Spartan,* not the *Roman,* though both for this respect
so much prais'd by the wise *Polybius,* more divinely and
harmoniously tun'd, more equally ballanc'd as it were by
the hand and scale of Justice, then is the Common-wealth
of *England:* where under a free, and untutor'd *Monarch,* the
noblest, worthiest, and most prudent men, with full appro-

---

27. *Works,* III, 63.
28. In the first two chapters of his *Classical Republicans* Professor Fink
traces the theory of mixed government from Polybius to its popular revival
in Tudor and Stuart England; see especially pp. 21-27.

bation, and suffrage of the People have in their power the supreame, and finall determination of highest Affaires.[29]

Milton's application here of the Polybian criterion for excellence in government implies acceptance, at least in principle, of Polybius' views; and that, even without further evidence, would commit Milton to a literal acceptance of the analogy we have just been examining. For Polybius regarded the true state as an organism with a natural life span of its own.[30] He described the natural development of that state as a cyclic sequence of six kinds of constitution, of which three are good and three degenerate.[31] Each desirable kind of constitution, he said, must be followed by the corresponding degenerate kind, so that the whole sequence from anarchy to anarchy naturally includes three lesser cycles of generation, bloom, and decay; at the conclusion of all these, society has no other course but to dissolve rapidly into formless savagery. Yet, convinced as Polybius was that no "pure" form of constitution can long avoid change, he was compelled to admit that Sparta and Rome had managed to maintain relative stability for an unusually long time; and he explained this stability as the natural result of a nice balance of political elements—king, lords, and commons—which these two states had managed to achieve in their constitutions. Thus did Polybius pursue his analysis of the state as a living organism with beautiful consistency, for the balance which he descried and praised in Sparta and Rome was strictly analogous to that balance of humors in the human body which alone could enable a man to enjoy health and long life.

29. *Works*, III, 63.
30. For Polybius' discussion see his *Histories* VI.3-9. All references to Polybius' work are to the six-volume edition and translation by W. R. Paton, Loeb Classical Library (London, 1922-1927).
31. These six kinds, in the order of their occurrence, are true kingship, monarchy (or tyranny), aristocracy, oligarchy, democracy, and mob-rule.

But with a consistency which was ultimately to prove uncomfortable for Milton, Polybius carried his analogy one step farther. Of his principal subject, Rome, he wrote: ". . . this state, more than any other, has been formed and has grown naturally, and will undergo a natural decline and change to its contrary."[32] This, it may be noted, is substantially what Plato had said about his own ideal constitution, the timocracy, based on love of honor: ". . . since for everything that has come into being destruction is appointed, not even such a fabric as this will abide for all time, but it shall surely be dissolved. . . ."[33] Neither Polybius nor Plato, however, seems to have seen anything alarming about such a conclusion. To the Greek, who habitually viewed most things in a hylozoistic fashion, decay was a matter of course, to be feared (if at all) only when it seemed imminent.

To Milton, on the other hand, it was almost sacrilege to believe that the English commonwealth, "more divinely and harmoniously tun'd, more equally ballanc'd . . . by the hand and scale of Justice" than any other civil government past or present, should have to undergo decay. Yet in spite of this, the possibility of decay was definitely haunting him in 1641. Having defined England as a mixed government in which "under a free, and untutor'd *Monarch*, the noblest, worthiest, and most prudent men, with full approbation, and suffrage of the People have in their power the supreame, and finall determination of highest Affaires," he had to face the chance that some intrusive element, like prelacy, might upset the delicate balance and send the state sliding down to democracy.[34] This was a danger that Polybius had described

32. *Histories* VI.9.
33. *The Republic* VIII.iii, trans. Paul Shorey, Loeb Classical Library (London, 1935), II, 245. Plato's discussion in this book of the *Republic* is probably the principal source of Polybius' political theory. Cf. also Aristotle *Politics* III.vii *et seq.*
34. *Works*, III, 57. Cf. Aristotle *Politics* III.xv.

in great detail and one that Milton obviously had in mind
when he described prelacy as having ever been "to our state
a continuall *Hydra* of Mischiefe, and molestation, the forge
of discord and Rebellion."[35] A second possible cause of
decay, equally fearful to think about, was that one or more
of the natural political elements might grow careless in well-
being, forget to be watchful of the state's spiritual and moral
integrity, and allow a fatal rot of wickedness and indifference to develop within the body politic. This possibility had
also given Milton a reason for denying the prelates any
share of temporal power. As he declared in *Of Reformation,*
"ever since their comming to the See of *Canterbury* for neere
twelve hundred yeares, to speake of them in generall, they
have beene in *England* to our Soules a sad and dolefull suc-
cession of illiterate and blind guides."[36] Having failed to
achieve virtue themselves, the prelates had taken no heed
that their people become virtuous; and the state when under their influence had periodically suffered the decay that
Milton considered to be the natural consequence both of
ill-health and of human sinning.

These two potential causes of decay were, of course,
within man's power to control, God willing and helping;
but apparently they were the source of greatest concern to
Milton when he came to write *Of Reformation* in 1641. His
prayer concluding that work shows them significantly linked
together: ". . . let not the obstinacy of our halfe Obedience
and will-Worship bring forth that *Viper* of *Sedition,* that for
these Fourescore Yeares hath been breeding to eat through
the entrals of our *Peace.* . . ."[37] Prelacy, the intrusive element, having made repeated assaults, was now ready to
strike her final blow; and the nation's moral laxity and

35. *Works,* III, 67. Cf. Polybius *Histories* VI.57.
36. *Works,* III, 67.
37. *Works,* III, 77. The prayer begins at p. 76.

indifference, in which lay prelacy's surest hope of success, was increasing with alarming rapidity. One immediately notes here that the tone of the prayer differs markedly from that passage previously quoted in which Milton asserted the superiority of the English commonwealth to those of Sparta and Rome. Instead of civil government divinely tuned, we now hear of a "travailling & throbbing Kingdome" and "this our shaken *Monarchy*, that now lies labouring under her throwes, and struggling against the grudges of more dreaded Calamities." But we are not to conclude from these phrases that Milton has abruptly changed his attitude toward the English body politic. Indeed, the prayer affirms that God has already brought the body politic itself virtually to the point of perfection and asks simply that it be kept there:

O thou that after the impetuous rage of five bloody Inundations, and the succeeding Sword of intestine *Warre,* soaking the Land in her owne gore, didst pitty the sad and ceasles revolution of our swift and thick-comming sorrowes when wee were quite breathlesse, of thy *free grace* didst motion *Peace,* and termes of Cov'nant with us, & having first welnigh freed us from *Antichristian* thraldome, didst build up this *Britannick Empire* to a glorious and enviable heighth with all her Daughter Ilands about her, stay us in this felicitie. . . .[38]

All that remains to be accomplished, once the dangers of prelacy and human indifference have been removed, is the union of honest Englishmen "to the *Prerogative* of thy eternall *Throne*."

The most important cause of decay in commonwealths, their natural tendency as living organisms, appears not to

38. The problem of identifying the five inundations referred to here will be dealt with in a more extended study treating of Milton's conception of history.

have troubled Milton when he wrote *Of Reformation.* For
one reason, he had his confidence in England's election to
spare him this fear. God had intervened, taken pity on the
"sad and ceasles revolution" of England's "swift and thick-
comming sorrowes," and of His free grace motioned peace
for the chosen commonwealth. Thus, decay, if it was to
come, would have to be the result of faithlessness and negli-
gence. Moreover, Milton shared the belief of many of his
contemporaries that the day was at hand when the "shortly-
expected King shalt open the Clouds to judge the severall
Kingdomes of the World."[39] It may well have occurred to
him that, election or no election, there was hardly time left
for any natural decay to complete its work.

III

Time unfortunately has a way of running out; and the
months that passed after the publication of *Of Reformation*
in 1641 brought, not a "shortly-expected King," but an increasing number of signs to indicate that natural decay was
imminent, or perhaps actually taking place. Nevertheless,
during these months and at least until after he had written
Areopagitica in 1644, Milton held fast to his conviction that
God had somehow miraculously intervened in the natural
processes of the English body politic to preserve it whole
for His use in the last days. Holding fast to that conviction,
however, made it imperative that Milton modify to some
extent his concept of the English constitution.

The solution which he hit upon may have been suggested
to him by Aristotle's *De generatione.*[40] There Aristotle explained that the cyclical sequences of the lower bodies
(which, according to Plato, were created mortal and cor-

39. *Works,* III, 78.
40. *De generatione et corruptione* II.xi.338A-338B.

rupt by the star-gods and not by God himself)[41] differ from
those of the heavenly bodies in one very important way:
heavenly bodies, being of an imperishable substance, can
remain numerically the same throughout the whole course
of a cycle, and cycle after cycle; while lower bodies, including man, are essentially perishable and can recur only in
species. Now, whether or not the suggestion for it had come
from Aristotle, Milton's modification of his Polybian description of the English commonwealth amounted to nothing
more than declaring the substance of that particular body
politic imperishable rather than perishable. Thus, whenever
events in England should force him to acknowledge that a
major change had occurred, he could conveniently deny that
the change was a prelude to dissolution and death. Whatever the timid might say, it was simply the prelude to a new
youth.

The best illustration of Milton's modified concept of the
English body politic is to be found in the familiar admonition
of Parliament in *Areopagitica:*

For as in a body, when the blood is fresh, the spirits pure
and vigorous, not only to vital, but to rational faculties, and
those in the acutest, and the pertest operations of wit and
suttlety, it argues in what good plight and constitution the
body is, so when the cherfulnesse of the people is so sprightly
up, as that it has, not only wherewith to guard well its own
freedom and safety, but to spare, and to bestow upon the
solidest and sublimest points of controversie, and new invention, it betok'ns us not degenerated, nor drooping to a
fatall decay, but casting off the old and wrincl'd skin of cor-
ruption to outlive these pangs and wax young again, entring
the glorious waies of Truth and prosperous vertue destin'd
to become great and honourable in these latter ages.[42]

41. *Timaeus* 69C.
42. See *Works*, IV, 344 ff.

Here was an explanation of the situation, together with proof. And what better proof of the youthfulness of a people's condition could there be than the vigor of their curiosity and disputatiousness? Yet, fearing perhaps that some of his more timid compatriots still might doubt, Milton hastened to strengthen his point by using as analogies two familiar cycles which even in mortal creatures could not be regarded as fatal: the salutary cycle of sleep and the moulting cycle of birds. With the first of these he brought in a forceful allusion to the biblical Samson, who experienced the effects of a somewhat analogous cycle when he inadvertently lost his hair: "Methinks I see in my mind a noble and puissant Nation rousing herself like a strong man after sleep, and shaking her invincible locks. . . ." The second was considerably more elaborate and considerably more to the point:

Methinks I see her as an Eagle muing her mighty youth, and kindling her undazl'd eyes at the full midday beam; purging and unscaling her long abused sight at the fountain itself of heav'nly radiance; while the whole noise of timorous and flocking birds, with those also that love the twilight, flutter about, amaz'd at what she means, and in their envious gabble would prognosticat a year of sects and schisms.[43]

In short, England, for all her seeming distress, was merely at the turning point of a cycle which, through God's special providence, could not end in dissolution.

The very explicitness of Milton's statement here, however, may indicate a weakening of his conviction. It was in 1641

43. In an interesting article, "The Word 'Muing' in Milton's *Areopagitica* (1644)," *RES*, XIX (1943), 61-66, Mr. G. Udny Yle has set forth his reasons for believing that Milton's "muing" in the passage quoted above is a misprint for "renuing." The sentence thus corrected would read: "Methinks I see her as an Eagle renuing her mighty youth," etc. This reading, if correct, supports my suggestion about Milton's use of both figures.

that he had first written of England's "casting farre from her the rags of her old vices."[44] If now in 1644 England was *still* at the turning point, she had been wavering there more than three years! Perhaps it pained him a little to recall with what confidence during those months before the war began he had attacked the doctrine of natural decay and predicted the immediate renewal of life for the commonwealth at the arrival of their "shortly-expected King." In *Animadversions* he had written: ". . . thy grace is not past away with the primitive times, as fond and faithless men imagine, but thy Kingdome is now at hand, and thou standing at the dore."[45] As he saw it then, regeneration was at hand:

Come forth out of thy Royall Chambers, O Prince of all the Kings of the earth, put on the visible roabes of thy imperiall Majesty, take up that unlimited Scepter which thy Almighty Father hath bequeath'd thee; for now the voice of thy Bride calls thee, and all creatures sigh to bee renew'd.[46]

The spirit of those pamphlets which Milton wrote in 1642 also gives evidence of faith and confidence. In that year he was able to write that the men of the Long Parliament were God's appointed to effect "the recovery of decay'd religion and the Common-wealth"; for these two causes, he said, "God hath inseparably knit together, and hath disclos'd to us that they who seek to corrupt our religion are the same that would inthrall our civil liberty."[47] It still seemed then "as if some divine commission from heav'n were descended to take into hearing and comiseration the long remedilesse afflictions of this kingdome."[48] When we think of the events that followed these expressions of hope, we find it easier to

44. *Works*, III, 78.
45. *Works*, III, 148.
46. *Ibid.*
47. *Apology for Smectymnuus*, in *Works*, III, 335-336.
48. *Works*, III, 340.

understand the dark coloring of despair that characterizes several passages in *Areopagitica;* for in 1644 Milton must have felt desperate indeed at having to remind these same men of what God for two years had been trying to do through them. "We reck'n more then five months yet to harvest; there need not be five weeks," he cried out; "had we but eyes to lift up, the fields are white already."[49] Yet the wheel continued to turn, as Milton later admitted in that digression on Parliament which he wrote into Book III of his *History of Britain;* the body politic did decay; and almost five years went by before he again took courage to hope that his England might achieve something worthy of an intelligent critic's praise.

In a very real sense, therefore, *Areopagitica* is the last work of Milton's political immaturity; for it is the last work in which he looked at contemporary events through the framework of a private political theory that postulated all normal earthly commonwealths by nature mortal and at the same time required him to expect some immediate divine recognition of England's immortality. With such a theory as this dominating his interpretation of events during the early 1640's, it is not surprising that the specter of civil decay tormented him whenever things seemed to be going badly. More often than not, unless he could convince himself that some sort of miraculous intervention had occurred or was about to occur, he had no alternative but to expect that England would undergo a normal political decline. And to expect this, at least until 1644, he steadfastly refused. The Milton who appeared in defense of regicide in 1649, however, had made a second study of English history; he had also reconsidered his theology and arrived at views which he believed could not be shaken; and he had evolved a new conception of history which left God's plan to devout specu-

49. *Works*, IV, 341.

lators and took more account of concrete facts. It is this new conception, less sanguine than the old one but more reliable, which appears in the defences, in *Paradise Lost,* and, above all, in the long-delayed *History of Britain.* And it is in the last of these—in a very real sense the first work of his maturity—that we find the solid statement of Milton's final views on the phenomenon of civil decay and the role of God's providence in human affairs. These subjects, however, are too large and complicated for consideration here and must be reserved for future studies.

ROBERT H. WEST

The Substance of Milton's Angels *

I

ONE OF THE UNRESOLVED CONTRADICTIONS
in *Paradise Lost* has to do with the substance of
the angels. On the one hand, they show themselves to Adam and Eve in their proper persons, not "in
mist"; they can assimilate human food; and they share one
first matter with the rest of creation. On the other hand,
they are called "pure Spirits," "incorporeal spirits"; they can
melt into each other without hindrance; and Raphael says
that to describe the war in heaven he must liken "spiritual
to corporal forms," implying, as it is supposed, that he will
put abstract activities of abstract beings into metaphor.

Professor Harris Fletcher says that Milton's angelology is
highly eclectic and so loose that the difficulties about substance are of the same order as the "vacillation" between the
Ptolemaic and Copernican cosmologies.[1] Mr. Grant Mc-
Colley, who asserts that Milton used three separate notions
of angelic substance and who cites parallels from extremely

* This article was made possible in part through a grant-in-aid, allocated
by a research committee at the University of Georgia from funds made
available jointly by the Carnegie Foundation and that university. The
author, however, is solely responsible for the statements made.

1. Harris Fletcher, *Milton's Rabbinical Readings* (Urbana, Ill., 1930),
pp. 217-218.

various demonologists,[2] seems to support Professor Fletcher's contention, as in part does Mr. P. L. Carver, who tries to show that Milton followed both materialist opinions of Tertullian and opposed opinions of Aquinas.

Mr. Carver feels, however, that in spite of this divergence of sources Milton would not have been willing to concede that his angelology was "only poetically true."[3] In this Mr. Carver anticipates Mr. C. S. Lewis, who, though admitting that a single passage may be discrepant, thinks that Milton is saying in *Paradise Lost* what he believed to be the real probability about angelic substance and is definitely on the materialist side.[4] Mr. E. M. W. Tillyard thinks Milton genuinely interested in angels and bent on using them to back his general materialism,[5] and Professor W. C. Curry has a related view.[6] M. Denis Saurat and Miss Marjorie H. Nicolson show Milton's alliances with particular Platonist demonologists.[7] Professor George Coffin Taylor, though not directly concerned with the question of substance, pleads the resemblance of Milton's treatment of angelic apparition to that of Du Bartas, whose idea about it was scholastic.[8]

Most of these authorities have written of angels only incidentally, some of them for no more than a paragraph or so, and few have been able to pay much attention to seventeenth-century angelology. The purpose of this article is to show by a relatively extensive examination of the angelology

2. Grant McColley, *Paradise Lost: The Birth of an Epic* (Chicago, 1940), pp. 112-113.

3. P. L. Carver, "The Angels in *Paradise Lost*," *RES*, XVI (1940), 417.

4. C. S. Lewis, *A Preface to Paradise Lost* (New York, 1942), ch. xv.

5. E. M. W. Tillyard, *Milton* (London, 1946), p. 229.

6. W. C. Curry, "Milton's Scale of Nature," *Stanford Studies in Language and Literature* (1941), pp. 173 ff.

7. In *Milton Man and Thinker* (London, 1946), III, i, Saurat notes parallels between Milton and Fludd. In "The Spirit World of Milton and More," *SP*, XXII (1925), 433, Miss Nicolson shows *PL*'s repeated similarities to Henry More's *Immortality of the Soul*.

8. George Coffin Taylor, *Milton's Use of Du Bartas* (Cambridge, 1934), p. 46.

in close comparison with *Paradise Lost*, that, given the kind of composition *Paradise Lost* is, Milton is not inconsistent in his portrayal of the angelic nature, but throughout rejects the scholastic opinion of angelic being and apparition, and broadly allies himself to the materialists as represented by Platonists and occultists like Henry More and Robert Fludd and by various Calvinist theologians.

I do not claim, of course, that what Milton says of angels in *Paradise Lost* is simply such a versification of authorities as is to be found in *The Works and Weeks* and *The Hierarchie of the Blessed Angels*. Since Milton's narrative is far more dramatic and tightly knit than Du Bartas' or Heywood's, with much less of pure exposition and much greater creative latitude, Milton suited his angels to his fiction not only in their personal traits but in their generic ones. The passage on Satan as a "stripling cherub," for instance, seems in positing youth and age among angels to be entirely outside angelology and, in a sense, above it.[9]

On the other hand, Milton did not allow himself so much freedom of this sort as did Tasso or Spenser. Mr. Tillyard thus describes Milton's general bent in composing *Paradise Lost*: Milton "allowed his ambitions to project themselves less into the remoter academic strictness of Vida's *Christiad* and Tasso's *Jerusalem Delivered* than into the immensely popular scientific and Protestant didacticism of Sylvester's huge translation."[10]

In the portrayal of the angels this bent shows itself in some expository passages as "technical" as anything in Heywood. Thus, as I have contended elsewhere,[11] Milton borrows in detail from Michael Psellus, a demonologist very

9. Some demonologists—Cardan and Paracelsus perhaps the best known—talk of differences in age among demons. They do not mean the inhabitants of heaven or hell, however, but elemental spirits.

10. E. M. W. Tillyard, *The Miltonic Setting* (London, 1947), pp. 172-173.

11. Robert H. West, "Milton and Michael Psellus," *PQ*, XXVII (1949).

widely known in the seventeenth century, when he represents angels as "pan-organic" with power to change size,
shape, and color, and to heal instantly injuries in their substance. Similarly Mr. Carver has pointed out that in the
passage on the apparition of Raphael, Milton takes sides
explicitly against scholastic angelologists. Mr. Carver thinks
it inconceivable that he should do this so roundly if the
question were indifferent to his purpose in *Paradise Lost*.[12]
Plainly, Milton does want, sometimes at least, to validate
his angels in the eyes of those who know the theory of
angels, to establish his treatment with its fit audience as an
acceptable "scientific and Protestant didacticism."

Milton was not committed to Psellus as doctrine, of course,
nor could his consistent alliance with the materialists have
put him, as Mr. A. J. A. Waldock scoffingly suggests,[13] in
danger of the stake. Milton's use of Psellus was largely literary opportunism, and probably no one in Milton's England received as essential to the Christian faith any single
speculation on the angelic substance. On the other hand,
this tolerance and this opportunism are no evidence that
Milton took the matter lightly enough to contradict himself
on it. The positiveness and the detail with which he asserts
Raphael's true apparition and ability to assimilate earthly
food are indication that he probably took the question of
angelic substance seriously enough to want consistency in
his answer. What he said about angelic substance was not
doctrine, but it was "science" in which he could hardly afford to be irresponsible.[14] Milton's age, as Mr. C. M. Bowra
says, "expected poetry to give information on most matters

12. Carver, p. 417.
13. A. J. A. Waldock, *Paradise Lost and its Critics* (New York, 1945),
p. 107.
14. If this needs arguing, see M. E. Prior, "Joseph Glanvill, Witchcraft,
and Seventeenth-Century Science," *MP*, XXX (1932).

of importance."[15] Milton was not the man to disappoint such an expectation.

II

In the seventeenth century three schools of thought on angelic substance are distinguishable among those who, like Milton, regarded angels as personal beings. Henry More summarizes: "Concerning angels, some affirm them to be *fiery* or *airy Bodies;* some pure spirits; some Spirits in airy or fiery bodies. . . ." The first class here consisted of those who followed the Platonized improvisations of the Fathers, and among sixteenth- and seventeenth-century writers comprised chiefly Calvinist theologians, of whom Jerome Zanchy was the most voluminous on angels, backed in England by such writers as Henry Lawrence and Isaac Ambrose. The second class comprises those who followed the superbly detailed scholastic rationalizations; it included most Catholic angelologists and perhaps a majority of Protestant ones. The third class, to which More himself belonged, is composed of those whom Mr. Lewis designates Platonists. During Milton's life this class consisted most prominently of the Cambridge group and of occultists like Robert Fludd.[16]

The scholastic position, as is well known, was that angels were simple intellectual substances, who sometimes manifested themselves to man by "assumed bodies," which they contrived for the moment out of the elements through an ordinary power, and which they managed but did not vital-

15. C. M. Bowra, *From Virgil to Milton* (New York, 1945), p. 238.

16. Such a classification as I have made here overlooks many details, of course, and it also obscures the very important facts that most of the "Platonists" were ardent Christians, many of the "Scholastics" Protestants, and the "Calvinists" by no means all professing followers of Geneva. The terms, nevertheless, are generally usable labels for the doctrines concerned. The reference in More is *The Grand Mystery of Godliness* (London, 1660) I.iii.6.

ize. The insistence that the angel was not compound of form and matter preserved, the Scholastics argued, the continuity of created beings up to God, for if angels had body "there would be wanting incorporeal creatures."[17]

But the Platonists thought the gap from bodily to bodiless creatures itself startling,[18] and they filled it as they could with "spirits in . . . bodies," that is, angelic souls vitalizing natural bodies ordinarily imperceptible to human sense, though occasionally thickening to visibility or even tangibility.

The Calvinists felt in this angelology of the Platonists a dangerous pagan luxuriance such as that which in the Hermetic literature clothed the soul in various layers of "vehicles." In the angelology of the Scholastics they felt an equally abhorrent tendency to make the angel an intermediary between man and his God. The Calvinists' problem was how to keep the severe scholastic insistence upon the angel as a unitary being and at the same time not allow him much closer to God than man himself was. Their characteristic Protestant tactic was, of course, appeal to the early church, most of whose authorities had, unlike the Scholastics, believed angels bodily in one way or another, usually without ruling on whether they were dichotomous or not.[19]

17. This quotation is from a footnote by Alexander Ross, "the Aristotelian fundamentalist" of his day, as Professor Bush calls him, in his translation of Wolleb's *Compendium.* See *The Abridgment of Christian Divinity* (London, 1656), p. 51. Ross makes the same point in *Leviathan Drawn out with a Hook* (London, 1653), p. 35. See also John Salkeld, *Treatise of Angels* (London, 1613), p. 33, where it is given as "the reason of the Divines." Almost any scholastic-minded divine on angels will confirm Salkeld.

18. The Scholastics, contends More, left to their own dry subtleties have made all intellectual beings that are not grossly terrestrial, like man, to be purely immaterial. "Whereby they make a very hideous Chasme or gaping breech in the order of things. . . ." Preface to *The Immortality of the Soul* (London, 1659). George Rust, Joseph Glanvill, and others say the same thing.

19. Origen, for instance, touches, without trying to come to a conclusion on it, the problem of whether angels are souls or have souls. See *De principiis* III.viii.286 in Vol. IV of *The Ante-Nicene Fathers,* translated by Roberts and Donaldson (New York, 1903).

This doctrine in the Fathers was usually a muted Platonism. But Tertullian and others under dialectical pressures about the Incarnation and about how the angels ate with Abraham, added the distinctly Christian contention that angels' substance was so rarefied that to serve man's senses they required a temporary gross body added to them by special act of God.[20] Augustine, for instance, seems to have held this.[21] It was a clumsy doctrine, but serviceable enough for a theology that emphasized as the Calvinists did, the unknowability of the angelic nature and the impropriety of asking much about it.[22]

Now Milton, Puritan and man of the Renaissance, writing in the presence of these three shades of opinion, would have, we should expect, conscious bonds with both the Platonists and the Calvinists, but few or none with the Scholastics. In view of his open repudiation once of the key scholastic article on apparition, we might expect a consistent avoidance of Scholasticism. And in *Paradise Lost* this is just what we have.

We might also expect that, writing in his maturity, Milton would flirt with the Platonists where they could help solve his literary problems, but that for serious doctrine he would march with the Calvinists unless independent opinions of his own crossed theirs. Then we should expect those independent opinions to be stated uncompromisingly, though perhaps adroitly enough to keep poetic values more prominent than polemical ones.[23] And this too in *Paradise Lost* is just what we have.

20. See *Against Marcion* III.ix.328, 329, in Vol. III of *The Ante-Nicene Fathers.* For Calvin's version, see *Commentaries on the First Book of Moses Called Genesis,* on Genesis xviii.2.

21. See *The City of God* XIII.xxii.

22. See Calvin's *Institutes* (London, 1580) I.xiv.44 ff.

23. On how Milton skillfully subdues his heresies by his poetry in *PL,* see B. Rajan, *Paradise Lost and the Seventeenth Century Reader* (London, 1947), p. 33.

To confirm this reading of *Paradise Lost,* the first thing is
to show that those who have referred some of its terms and
passages on angelic substance to the Scholastics have not
looked far enough.

III

Milton's express rejection of scholastic angelology comes
in the passage about Raphael's eating with Adam:

> ... *nor seemingly*
> *The Angel, nor in mist, the common gloss*
> *Of Theologians, but with keen dispatch*
> *Of real hunger, and concoctive heate*
> *To transubstantiate; what redounds, transpires*
> *Through Spirits with ease....*
>
> (V.434-439)

Mr. Carver grants that this is aimed directly at the Scholastics, and thinks that "nor in mist" refers to an obscure
point in Duns Scotus that earthly food taken by angelic
apparitions was dissipated in fumes. Milton, Mr. Carver
feels, used the expression to emphasize his repudiation of
scholastic philosophy in the insistence that Raphael did not
just seem to eat. Undoubtedly the passage is a repudiation
of the Scholastics, but Milton rather accepts than rejects
Scotus' notion that food "transpires through spirits," except
that Milton is clearly speaking here of the angelical essence
whereas Scotus meant the assumed body, and that Milton
says it is only the redundant food that transpires whereas to
Scotus all was redundant. By "... nor seemingly the Angel,
nor in mist, ..." Milton means that Raphael does not just
seem to be present—that is, in assumed body, "in mist," as
the "Theologians" have it—but is genuinely there in his
proper person and so truly eats. The passage invites this
construction, and as a repudiation of "the common gloss" it

is far stronger than Mr. Carver's construction, for it sweeps away not merely a special item in the work of a single "Theologian" but the whole of Scholasticism's focal and widely known rationalization on angelic apparition.[24]

Now, if alongside this pointed dismissal Milton anywhere uses the scholastic idea of angelic substance as pure spirit, he has indeed gone senselessly out of his way.

Mr. Carver indicates that one sign of Thomism in *Paradise Lost* is that Adam "acknowledges" Raphael to be a "pure intelligence" (VIII.180). Mr. Carver seems to think that no accommodation of such a phrase is possible, but simply that Milton's conception of angels is split between Tertullian's and Aquinas'.[25] Verity had quoted "incorporeal Spirits" (I.789) with the same sort of implication,[26] and similar expressions are plentiful: "Spiritual substance" (IV.585), "spiritual . . . forms" (V.573), "purest Spirits" (V.406), "pure/Intelligential substances" (V.407-408).

In Milton's time, however, the word *spirit* applied to angels did not necessarily contradict the words *body* and *matter*, and this confusing usage appears in virtually every demonologist who tries to ascribe body to angels. Psellus, perhaps the most widely cited of such writers, says with what to us seems ambiguity that the "body which angels

---

24. That the assumed bodies were usually of vaporized air, that is, of clouds or "mist," is an inescapable commonplace among the dozens of angelologists who stop to expound the scholastic notion. See, for instance, *Angels* (Amsterdam, 1646), p. 15; Pierre Le Loyer, *A Treatise of Specters* (London, 1658), p. 363; Strozzio Cicogna, *Magiae omnifariae* (Cologne, 1607) III.ii.293; Henry Lawrence, *Of our Communion and Warre with Angels* (Amsterdam, 1646), p. 15; Pierre Le Loyer, *A Treatise of Specters* (London, 1605) v.45; R. P. Maldonat, *Traicté des Anges et Démons* (Paris, 1605) iv.26; John Salkeld, *A Treatise of Angels* (London, 1613) viii.39; François Perreaud, *Démonologie* (Geneva, 1653) ix.140; and of course Aquinas, *Summa theologica* Q. 51, Art. II. Possible references on this point are almost innumerable.

25. Carver, p. 430.

26. Note to I.777-780, in his edition of *PL*.

have" is "immaterial."[27] Cornelius Agrippa, a beacon light
to many Platonists of the Renaissance, can state blandly
that 'Angelicall spirits" are "altogether incorporeal,"[28] and
Robert Fludd in the midst of an angry argument to prove
devils corporeal yet speaks of their "spiritual substance,"
actually meaning the stuff of their bodies.[29] Henry More,
who made prodigious efforts, mostly from the Platonist point
of view, to clarify the conception of spirits, calls angels "pure
spirits" yet with bodies.[30] In another place they are "immaterial substance," on the same page on which he speaks
of their bodies.[31] A little later in the same treatise he says
that he agrees with some who call spirits material, though
he will insist that they miscall them.[32] Zanchy, who sharply
snubs the scholastic opinion and was generally acknowledged to stand with those who held for body in angels,
can say at the start of his argument that, as is the opinion
of nearly all, angels are incorporeal substances of a spiritual
nature and free of all matter.[33]

Plainly, then, when Milton speaks of angels as "spirits"
he is not necessarily contradicting what he also says in some
places of their bodiliness. The Bible tells us, he says in
Christian Doctrine, "what a spirit is, or rather what it is
not ... Luke xxiv.39. 'a spirit hath not flesh and bones.' "[34]
Milton certainly shows his angels free of flesh and bones.

27. See p. 29 of Marcus Collison's translation, *Psellus' Dialogue on the Operation of Daemons* (Sidney, 1848). For Renaissance translations see Pierre Moreau's *Traicté par Dialogue de l'Energie ou Opération des Diables* (Paris? *ca.* 1578) viii.17, and Ficino's *De daemonibus* (Lyons, 1577), p. 335.
28. Cornelius Agrippa, *Occult Philosophy* (London, 1651) III.xxx.444.
29. Robert Fludd, *Answer unto M. Foster* (London, 1631) III.vi.54.
30. Henry More, appendix to *The Antidote against Atheism,* ch. xiii, p. 223, in *Several Philosophical Writings* (London, 1712).
31. Henry More, *An Answer to a Letter of a Learned Psychopyrist* xv.133, in *Sadducismus triumphatus* (London, 1726).
32. More, *Answer* xvi.135.
33. Jerome Zanchy, *De operibus Dei* I.II.i.59 in Vol. III of *Operum theologicorum* (Geneva, 1613).
34. I.ii, in Milton's *Works,* ed. F. A. Patterson, Columbia edition (New York, 1931-1938), XIV, 41.

But this does not mean they are without a simple and tenuous matter. The bodies of Adam and Eve, says Raphael, may in time "turn all to spirit," that is, may "wingd ascend Ethereal" like angels (V.496-498). Here spirit and ether are plainly equated, and ether was, in the almost universal opinion of angelologists, a kind of matter.

The grounds of the verbal confusion among angelologists are two. First is the well-known conception that subtile bodies were "immaterial" and "incorporeal" in the sense that they had no gross matter or bodily members. When Agrippa says that an angel is an "Intelligence . . . free from all gross and putrefying mass of body," it is no denial that the angel has a refined and incorruptible tenuity of body; Fludd uses identical phraseology with the same intention.[35] Further, in a polemical work Fludd asks rhetorically about his opponent: "Doth he think that the very ayre (which is the externall of the Deuill as shall be proued) is not a spiritual body, when it may be felt, heard, or understood, though not as flesh and bones?"[36] The Calvinist Isaac Ambrose says that compared with men angels are "pure . . . spirits."[37]

In the second place, confusion arises from the fact that besides speaking sometimes of a rarefied body as though it were itself spiritual and at others insisting on its materiality, the Platonists talk also of the angel's "soul" or "internal," the "principle" of his tenuous "vehicle" or "external," and against a materialist such as Hobbes they insist fervently that the "internal" is spiritual in a sense that separates it from all matter. Thus, More says that to suppose no created spirit incorporeal in any sense save that of tenuity is error.[38] Again, sometimes the Platonists talk of the angel as a total being,

---

35. Agrippa III.xvi.390; Fludd, *Utriusque cosmi historia* (Frankfurt, 1617-1623) I.IV.i.108.

36. Fludd, *Answer* III.vi.48.

37. Isaac Ambrose, *Communion with Angels* I.ii.103 in *Compleat Works* (1674). The *Communion* was first published in 1661.

38. More, *Answer* xvi.135.

internal and external together, and call him spirit, though wholly without prejudice to his external bodiliness.[39]

All these latitudes, however, are confined to the Platonists and the Calvinists, who need them to explain scriptural references to angels as spirits. The Scholastics say repeatedly that body and spirit are antithetical and that angels have no body.[40] Milton, consequently, is either showing consistently a Platonic or Calvinistic looseness of terminology in one way or another, or he is confusing by a scholastic terminology a conception that no one denies to be largely antischolastic. The evidence that in some passages he conceived his angels to be or to have body is overwhelming, whereas the evidence that he anywhere conceived his angels as without body is slim. In fact, *Paradise Lost* has no passage in which the concept of tenuous body does not explain adequately all the traits referable to the substance of its angels, —the traits, that is, which are explicable at all in angelology.

IV

Milton's first considerable expository passage on the angels he borrows in content from Psellus:

39. A further confusion is that the Platonists do occasionally refer to angels that they hold to be separated substances in approximately the scholastic sense. Thus Agrippa on those angels revolving around God (*Occult Philosophy* III.xvi.390) and More in *The Grand Mystery of Godliness* (London, 1660) II.iii.34 on *Noes* and *Enades*. Neither man gives much consideration to such beings, for according to Agrippa they do not intervene on earth, and More only reports them from the ancients, does not vouch for them. Agrippa mentions also the abstractions, Love and Sleep, following Apuleius in *The God of Socrates*, as immaterial spirits (III.xix.402), as does Jacob Boissard, *De divinatione et magicis* (Oppenheim, 1616), "De Magia" x.74. Glanvill, Cudworth, and others mention the *Enades* without much interest.

40. Almost no one denied an absolute distinction between body and spirit as substances. The question about angels was simply, body or spirit or both? and if body, what degree of it? The Platonists and the Calvinists appeal as feelingly as the Scholastics to the distinctions of spirit and body. See Peter Martyr, *The Common Places* (London, 1574) I.x.81, and Benjamin Camfield, *Discourse of Angels* (London, 1678) ii.12.13.

> *. . . For Spirits when they please*
> *Can either Sex assume, or both; so soft*
> *And uncompounded is thir Essence pure,*
> *Not ti'd or manacl'd with joint or limb,*
> *Nor founded on the brittle strength of bones,*
> *Like cumbrous flesh; but in what shape they choose*
> *Dilated or condenst, bright or obscure,*
> *Can execute thir aerie purposes,*
> *And works of love or enmity fulfill.*
>
> (I.423-431)

Mr. Grant McColley, taking no notice of the indebtedness to Psellus which Newton had pointed out, says that in this passage Milton "sets forth" the "traditional conception" of "all spirits as non-corporeal" in contradistinction to that which Raphael gives in his explanation of angels' eating. To show that he has justly stated the "traditional conception" Mr. McColley cites Thomas Heywood to the effect that "the best theologians assert" angels incorporeal; and then to show that Milton's passage is in this tradition he quotes the anonymous second book appended to the 1665 edition of Reginald Scot's *Discourse Concerning Devils and Spirits* as saying that spirits have power to expand and contract.[41]

Mr. McColley is no doubt right that the Thomistic was the dominant tradition—though Heywood's saying that the "best theologians" hold for incorporeity proves nothing but that he was of the party of those that did; Fludd, for instance, says exactly the reverse.[42] But the quotation from the *Discourse* does not show that Milton's passage was thus traditional, for this added book of the *Discourse* is a febrile hodgepodge of a sort of Paracelsan Platonism and is about

---

41. Scot, *Discourse,* p. 112.
42. Fludd, *Answer* III.vi.48.

as far from Scholasticism and its tradition as demonology could be.[43]

Mr. McColley further supposes that the passage in Book VI on Satan's wound and the pain it causes him—another patent borrowing from Psellus—is explained by a jeering echo of Psellus in that book of the *Discourse* which Scot himself wrote, and that somehow in a way not clear to me it represents yet a third conception of angelic substance, a "middle ground interpretation of the nature of spirits."[44]

But the two passages from Psellus are unquestionably alike and both on the Platonist side—that is, they talk about spirits with natural bodies. This follows not only from the universal reputation Psellus had among demonologists as a Platonist and one of the chief of those who ascribed body to spirits, but from the meaning of the passages themselves. When Milton and Psellus say that the substance of spirits is sexless because "uncompounded," they do not mean that it is form without matter, but simply that it is not differentiated into members;[45] and that this is the sense of it in *Paradise Lost* appears in the second passage in question (VI.327-353) when Milton, like Psellus, returns to the business of spirits' "liquid texture" and, like Psellus, explains that they are without organs: "All Heart they live, all Head, all Eye, all Eare,/all Intellect, all Sense...."

43. Paracelsan demonology was highly original in many ways. It is separated from the demonology of *PL* by the fact that Paracelsus is usually talking not about fallen angels but about nature spirits, which he held to be a separate genus entirely. See Franz Hartmann, *The Life of Paracelsus* (London, n.d.), ch. v, and *Paracelsus of the Supreme Mysteries of Nature* (London, 1655), translated by Robert Turner, iv.51, ff. Paracelsan demonology dominates *Le Comtes de Gabalis* and furnishes the machinery in the *Rape of the Lock*. There is hardly a whiff of it in all Milton.

44. Scot, p. 113. Mr. McColley's note refers us to *The Discovery of Witchcraft*, but apparently what he intends is the *Discourse* I.iii.

45. For a modern interpretation of Psellus on this, see K. Svoboda, *La Démonologie de Michel Psellos* (Brno, 1927), p. 20. On the eight kinds of composition recognized by theologians and which of them may be ascribed to angels, see the Jesuit R. P. Maldonat IV.iii.31 ff.

Professor Harris Fletcher suggests that Milton's passage on how angels embrace one another (VIII.615 ff.) shows Milton's angels to be "wholly spiritual," a phrase which, to judge by his preceding sketch of medieval angelology, he intends in a Thomistic sense.[46] True, Milton does seem to show a little reserve on the matter: Raphael gives no direct answer to Adam's question: ". . . do they mix/Irradiance, virtual or immediat touch?" Instead of confirming or denying the scholastic term *virtual*, Raphael says that for Adam it is enough to know angels happy, which they could not be without love. But this is apparently just a conventional Protestant rebuke to Scholasticism's too "curious" angelology, for Raphael does go on to describe angels' embraces. Evidently their contact is immediate, not virtual. Angels find no obstacle of membrane, joint, or limb, and mix more easily than air with air.

Nothing in this passage is incompatible with tenuous body, for its resemblance to Milton's Psellian description of the angelic essence—"Not ti'd or manacl'd with joint or limb,/Nor founded on the brittle strength of bones,/Like cumbrous flesh" (I.426-428)—is evident and Milton's very phrase, "Easier than Air with Air, if Spirits embrace,/Total they mix" (VIII.626) suggests not an absence of body, but a body more subtile than air—ether or the empyrean. M. Saurat quotes a passage from Robert Fludd in which angels are "essentia simplicissima, et quasi immaterialis, lucida, pura, distincta . . . eorum denique operatio, per quam exercentur, voluntaria est, subita, utilis et honesta, operantur enim sine retardatione aut impedimento."[47] True, this quotation says nothing specifically of the loving miscibility of angel with angel; but neither does any other that I have

46. Fletcher, p. 217.
47. See Saurat, p. 266.

been able to find.[48] The point here is that the embraces of
Milton's angels are as explicable in Platonic terms as in any.
Another and more general passage troubles Mr. Lewis as
a possible recession from materialism. It is the qualification
with which Raphael begins his story of the war in heaven:

>   *... how shall I relate*
> *To human sense th' invisible exploits*
> *Of warring Spirits? ...*
>   *... what surmounts the reach*
> *Of human sense, I shall delineat so,*
> *By lik'ning spiritual to corporeal forms,*
> *As may express them best, though what if Earth*
> *Be but the shaddow of Heav'n, and things therein*
> *Each to other like, more then on Earth is thought?*
>   (V.564-576)

Here, says Mr. Lewis, "Raphael seems to assume the
modern or scholastic view." Still, he goes on, by *corporeal*
Raphael may mean no more than "'grossly corporeal,' 'having
bodies like ours.' The adaptation which Raphael promises
may consist not in describing pure spirits as material, but in
describing the material, though strictly unimaginable, bodies
of angels as if they were fully human."[49] That this is what
Raphael does intend is indicated by his later exclamation:

>   *... for who, though with the tongue*
> *Of Angels, can relate, or to what things*
> *Lik'n on Earth conspicuous, that may lift*
> *Human imagination to such highth*
> *Of Godlike Power ...*
>   (VI.297-301)

48. Milton's idea that heavenly beings engaged in amorous embraces
with each other was, I believe, without close precedent in Renaissance
angelology. See Robert W. West, "Milton's Angelological Heresies," *JHI*,
XIV (1953), 116-123.
49. Lewis, p. 108.

His difficulty here is not that Satan and Michael are un-imaginable because they are abstract beings, but that their transcending prowess and glory and what Mr. Waldock calls the "Wellsian" conditions of their combat are totally unlike anything ever "conspicuous" to man. Raphael does not think of angels as free of "first matter," but simply acknowledges that in angels matter is in a form not ordinarily subject to man's senses. In *Christian Doctrine* Milton rather pointedly says that the highest heavens and the angels are the things God created invisible, *"at least . . . to us"*[50] [italics mine]. The clear implication is that heaven may have a kind of body, and things in heaven may be more like those on earth than on earth is thought.

The last argument for supposing that Milton sometimes contradicts himself with a scholastic conception of angelic substance is that in which Mr. Carver, showing many parallels between Milton's angelology and Aquinas', contends that one speech of angel to angel, contrasted with the speech of angel to man, is wholly free of metaphor and thus suggests that the speaker was a spirit in the Thomist sense.[51] Peter Martyr makes the point in angelology: ". . . the schoole diuines haue decreed, that . . . bicause those heauenlie minds haue no need of images or of senses . . . it should be superfluous for them to haue bodies."[52]

Mr. Carver may be correct in his assumption that the conspiratorial speech of Satan to "his next subordinate" (V.673) lacks metaphor because Milton is portraying angels as beings who understand intuitively; indeed, Raphael has said that intuitive reason belongs "most" to the angels (V.489). But it does not follow that Milton was using Aquinas; many Calvinists and Platonists had picked up this article together

50. *Christian Doctrine* I.vii, *Works*, XIV, 29.
51. Carver, pp. 423-425.
52. Martyr I.xiii.112. See also the *Commentary on Judges* (London, 1564), fol. 208b.

with most of the others Mr. Carver cites in *Paradise Lost* as
Thomistic, and they did it without admitting the Thomistic
inference that angels were bodiless.[53]

V

Needless to say, if the passages in *Paradise Lost* on angels'
apparition to men will not fit the scholastic rationalization
of a misty body contrived and managed by the angel's ordinary power, they fit still less the Calvinist notion that God
creates a gross body especially for each occasion. Nothing
in the poem suggests this scheme, and all the material from
Psellus suggests the Platonist idea of apparition by contraction of a natural body. Certainly the fact that Raphael's was
a body that hungered and that digested earthly food is as
much against the Calvinists as against the Scholastics, for
they all insist that angels who eat with men know neither
hunger nor nourishment.[54]

Milton's reasons for passing over the Calvinist idea were,
no doubt, largely literary: it would perhaps have been cum-
bersome; Milton could not have shifted his scene from
Heaven to the Garden as simply as he wished; he did not
want Raphael as an intolerably remote being with only a
blank and momentary special identity on earth. But his
reasons were also philosophical: evidently Milton was bent
on bringing in his idea of the scale of nature, and for it he
needed Raphael as he has him—a natural being with a full
set of native traits linking him very closely to man.

The ignoring of the Calvinist tenet on apparition does not
mean, however, that Milton totally rejects the Calvinists on
angelic substance as he does the Scholastics. The Calvinist
angelologists are as much distinguished by their reticence

53. Thus Fludd, *Utriusque* I.IV.xi.123; Zanchy III.vi.114; Lawrence, *Of
Our Communion and Warre with Angels* (Amsterdam, 1646), p. 30.
54. See West, "Milton's . . . Heresies."

on substance as by their tenets on it, and it is in their spirit
of stern humility, of reserve on whatever is not from Scripture, that Milton largely writes. It is the spirit of Augustine
and Bernard, who declare certain things about angels sure
from Scripture, but confess that whether angels have proper
bodies or not is too hard a question for them.[55] Similarly,
Jerome Zanchy, by far the most elaborate of the Calvinist
angelologists, refrains from a formal thesis on substance,[56]
and Heinrich Bullinger says that no man knows angels' nature truly.[57] In the seventeenth century Francois Perreaud,
a Swiss minister whose story of the demon of Mascon was
sponsored in England by Robert Boyle, sketches both the
scholastic and the Platonic speculations on substance, then
indicates that prolonged attention to them is not worth a
good man's while.[58] Henry Lawrence, the "virtuous father"
in Milton's twentieth sonnet, says in his respected book of
angels that the arguments of Schoolmen and philosophers
are worthy to pass the time, but that Scripture gives no issue
from them, so he will not trouble.[59] Isaac Ambrose thinks
that between the eccentricities of the Platonics and those
of the Scholastics a middle way is best.[60] And just so in
Christian Doctrine Milton has only a phrase or so for substance and brings up short his whole discussion of angels
with a text constantly in the mouths of the Calvinists against
presumptuous intrusion into those things which man has not
seen.[61]

In *Paradise Lost*, certainly, Milton does not retain all the

55. *Enchiridion* lix.217 in Vol. IX of *The Works of Aurelius Augustine*,
trans. Marcus Dods (Edinburgh, 1892). Bernard, *De consideratione* V.iv.453,
and *Sermones in Cantica Canticorum* v.1284 in Vol. I of *Opera Omnia*
(Paris, 1719).
56. Zanchy II.iii.
57. *The Decades of Henry Bullinger*, 9th Sermon, 4th Decade, p. 328.
58. Perreaud ix.136-137.
59. Lawrence, p. 9.
60. Ambrose ii.103.
61. I.vii, *Works*, XIV, 37. The text is Col. ii.18.

caution and spareness of the doctrinal treatise. He could not
have done so and written the epic as "scientific didacticism."
But that Milton was cold to angelological speculation as
such even in *Paradise Lost* is sugggested by the facts that
he has not a word on such prominent topics as how angels
are in place and whether they are dichotomous, that he
never uses any of the special terms of the famous English
angelologists of his day *(indiscerptible, dilatation, penetra-
ble, externum, alterity)*, and that his levy on Psellus is positive
but perfunctory.[62] True, in his explanation of Raphael's meal
with Adam he does become detailed in angelology and is certainly both beyond and against Calvinist doctrine. The same
holds for what he says of angels' love-making. But for Milton
the issue on angels' power to assimilate human food and to
"express thir love" was a larger one than anything in angelology; it had to do with the goodness of matter and its uni-
versality in created things.[63] Milton treats it with a Calvinist
gravity, clinging, it would seem, to the Bible statement that
angels "did eat" with Abraham—though he interprets that
statement for himself and not according to the orthodox
commentators, Calvinist or scholastic.

The pious reserve of the Calvinists on substance usually
issued in the inconclusive doctrine that angels were like the
body of the higher heavens: ". . . in comparison of God they
are bodies, but in comparison of us they are pure and mighty
spirits."[64] This was an ancient rationalization useful to all
parties. Aquinas cites it in Damascene and shows that though
in a sense acceptable it does not prevent one from saying that
angels are beings "without anything corporeal in them,"[65]

62. See West, "Milton and Michael Psellus."
63. See Rex Clements, "The Angels in *Paradise Lost*," *Quarterly Review*,
CCLXIV (1935), 285 ff., and Tillyard, *Milton*, p. 229. See also West,
"Milton's . . . Heresies."
64. Ambrose I.ii.103.
65. *Summa theologica*, Q. 50, Art. I, in *Basic Writings of Saint Thomas
Aquinas* (New York, 1945).

and Renaissance Scholastics such as Casman, Cicogna, and
Maldonat follow him.[66] In England scholastic-minded authorities such as Heywood and William Foster, a clergyman
who contended against Fludd, use the doctrine to excuse
those Fathers who speak as though angels had bodies.[67]
But Peter Martyr scornfully characterizes it, thus used, as
a mere evasion. It is the Scholastics, he feels, that need excuse, not the Fathers.[68] And so Ambrose, Zanchy, Lawrence,
John Webster, and others read it to signify corporeality.[69]

And so, it seems, does Milton in Raphael's explanation of
how "body up to spirit" works:

> *. . . one first matter all,*
> *Indu'd with various forms, various degrees*
> *Of substance, and in things that live, of life;*
> *But more refin'd, more spiritous, and pure,*
> *As neerer to him plac't or neerer tending. . . .*
> (V.472-476)

Linked with this is another resemblance between Milton
and the Calvinists, in the idea that the body of the angels

66. Otho Casman, *Angelographia* (Frankfurt, 1605) I.iii, pp. 62, 63;
Cicogna II.viii.195; Maldonat IV.i.20.

67. Thomas Heywood, *Hierarchie of the Blessed Angels* (London, 1635)
IV.210; Foster, *A Sponge to Wipe away the Weapon Salve* (London, 1629)
III.vi.50.

68. *Most Fruitful and Learned Commentaries of Dr. Peter Martyr* (London, 1564) on Judges xiii, fol. 209. See also *The Common Places* (London,
1574) I.xiii.113.

69. Zanchy II.iv.70; Lawrence, p. 9; Webster, *The Displaying of Supposed Witchcraft* (London, 1677) x.208. No doctrine was more turned
about than this one. Peter Martyr, who in one place sneers at the Scholastics' use of it to establish the immateriality of angels, in another place
uses it himself for exactly that purpose (*Common Places* I.x.81). Benjamin
Camfield, who follows More in contending that angels have bodies and
that the angel's "soul" is pure spirit, uses the doctrine to explain away
Fathers whom he supposes to think that angels *are* bodies (*Discourse* ii.21).
The heterodox Catholic Pierre Charron uses it to show that angels—and, of
more interest to him, the soul—are material in just the way Camfield opposes.
See *Of Wisedom* (London, 1630) I.vii.25, 26.

is of a substance called *ether* or the *empyrean*. In *Paradise Lost* the angels are without distinction "Ethereal substance" (VI.330), "Ethereal mould" (II.139), "Empyreal substance" (I.118), "Empyreal forme" (VI.433). That this substance itself is what Milton sometimes calls *spirit* is indicated by such passages as that in which Satan distinguishes Adam and Eve as "Creatures of other mould.../Not Spirits..." (IV. 360-361). In *Christian Doctrine,* too, the highest (or empyreal) heaven and the angels are the things God created invisible—"at least... to us."[70] And in *Paradise Lost* again, Heaven is in the Empyrean. This is the general Calvinist doctrine as Ambrose, for instance, gives it in an admiring paraphrase of Zanchy:

[Angels] *are not simply and altogether incorporeal, only their bodies* (saith Zanchy) *are not earthly, nor airy nor heavenly as the Stoicks would have them, for all such bodies were created of that Chaos* Gen.1.1 *but rather as the Empireal heaven is a corporeal substance far different from those neather heavens visible to us, so the angels made together with that heaven, are corporeal substance, far purer & more subtile than either earth or ayre or fire or the matter of these visible heavens.* I will not say that they are of the same body, but they may have like bodies to that glorious body of the highest heaven, or seat of the blessed; & so in respect of us and our crass bodies they may be called pure and mighty spirits.[71]

The "empyrean," then, of Zanchy and Ambrose is, like Milton's empyrean, the stuff of the superior heavens, an unearthly fire so different from the elements that though it is not spirit in the scholastic sense it is almost a third and intermediate substance. It is what Richard Baxter, disputing with Henry More on the nature of spirits, calls *Ignis emi-*

---

70. I.vii, *Works*, XIV, 29.
71. Ambrose I.ii.104.

nenter, and More acknowledges that this idea that finite spirits are of such quasi-material substance is very widespread.[72] Among Protestants even stout partisans of the scholastic opinion could find Zanchy's name so weighty as almost to force acknowledgment of a kind of body in angels. Thus John Deacon and John Walker, a pair of Church of England controversialists on demonic possession, support the scholastic ideas against Augustine and half a dozen others, then tamely admit the great authority of Zanchy's judgment that angels are probably corporeal. They insist, however, that the kind of body Zanchy settles on is so near spirit in its properties as to suit very well their particular contentions about possession.[73]

In some of his terms, then, and in their general implication Milton seems of the Calvinist way of thought, though his sally about angels eating earthly food is a drastic break with Calvinist thought.

VI

Between the Calvinists and the Platonists, both holding angels in some sense bodily, both claiming authority of Scripture and the Fathers, there is a considerable overlap of opinion, and they share many terms. No less than the Calvinists, the Platonists use Milton's *ethereal* and *empyreal* and the other words he applies to angels. But the Platonists do not mean just what the Calvinists seem to, for the Plato-

72. More, *Answer* xvi.135, 136. This is More's first answer to Baxter, who had given his views in a letter from which More's answer quotes freely. On *Ignis eminenter* see xx.141 ff. Baxter printed his original letter in his answer to More, *Of The Nature of Spirits* (London, 1682). More answered the answer in a 66-page digression in his *Annotations upon Lux Orientalis* (London, 1682). The argument is fearsomely intricate and often as unintelligible as those passages from Fludd which Richard Burthogge quoted as examples of what he meant by "nonsense."

73. John Deacon and John Walker, *A Dialogicall Discourse of Spirits and Devils* (London, 1601), iii.89-93.

nists ordinarily use these words with a distinction between the angel's essence and his "vehicle." Against Baxter, More says flatly that ether is *body* and in angels is the substance of the vehicle only. The Platonists have little of the Calvinist reticence. They confidently diagram what the Calvinists draw back from as mystery, and they particularly insist that angels are dichotomous.

Now, whether Milton follows the Platonists in this is perhaps impossible to say. The question of dichotomy was far less pressing for him than the practical one of whether angels could change size and shape, a question that he had to answer if he was to establish the most elementary correspondence between his angels and the general notion of angels. The matter of dichotomy seems also to be outside his special interest in the scale of nature. If, like the Platonists, Milton thought angels compounded of body and soul, he still felt no need to say so explicitly in *Paradise Lost*.

In *Christian Doctrine,* on the other hand, Milton is, perhaps, explicit about dichotomy. Angels, he says, "are spirits" and "of ethereal nature."[74] This laconic remark, backed with its proof texts, is nicely in the tone of Milton's presumed models, "the shorter systems" of Ames, Wolleb, and the rest; but it is also somewhat at odds with their matter, for not a single one of them in dealing with the invisible creation makes the controversial dual ascription to the angels of an ethereal nature plus their being as spirits.[75] Milton would seem here to be showing his usual independence in interpreting Scripture.

74. I.vii, *Works,* XIV, 35.
75. I have examined Ames's *Marrow of Sacred Divinity,* Wolleb's *Abridgment of Christian Divinity,* Ursinus' *The Summe of Christian Religion,* Musculus' *The Commonplaces of Christian Religion,* and Gomarus' *Disputationes theologicae,* plus, of course, the works of Calvin and Peter Martyr, thus covering the men mentioned by Edward Phillips as models for *Christian Doctrine* and most of the divines cited by Milton himself therein (II.vii, *Works,* XIV, 193) as among the "best."

But what he means is not clear. As proof texts for the ethereal nature he offers Psalm civ.4 and its echo in Hebrews i.7: "Who maketh his angels spirits and his ministers a flaming fire." In angelology these were among the most often cited biblical texts and among the most controversial. Psellus, for instance, notes that Basil inferred the materiality of angels from "flaming fire"; but the Scholastics explain away "flaming fire" and infer the pure spirituality of angels from the rest of the text.[76] By "flaming fire"—that is, ether—did Milton mean, like the Scholastics and many Calvinists, merely that the angels burned in beauty, zeal, and the love of God?[77] Nothing in *Christian Doctrine* positively forbids this figurative interpretation, but it will not do for *Paradise Lost* on Satan's "Ethereal substance . . ./Not long divisible" (VI.330-331) or for the "Ethereal mould/Incapable of stain" (II.139). Did Milton mean, then, that when angels come into the natural world God "cloatheth his angels with subtil bodies of wind or air, or fire as he sees fit"?[78] But this Calvinist doctrine of special apparition is clearly ignored in *Paradise Lost*; and besides, the passages just cited from *Paradise Lost* tell of angels in heaven and hell, not of angels come into the natural world.

Perhaps, then, in *Christian Doctrine* Milton does intend,

76. On Psellus, see the *Dialogue* as translated by Marcus Collison, p. 28. See also the opening paragraph of Ficino's Latin *De daemonibus*. Aquinas (*Summa theologica*, Q. 50, Art. I) and many who follow him cite Psalm civ.4 to prove angels spirits. When they mention "flaming fire," it is to interpret it figuratively.

77. For a summary of opinion on this text, see Camfield, p. 208 ff. He cites Gouge, Junius and Tremellius, Ainsworth, and others as giving figurative interpretations. He might also have mentioned Gomarus, Pt. I, p. 614, in the analysis of Hebrews i; John Amos Comenius, *Natural Philosophy Reformed by Divine Light* (London, 1651) xii.237; Christopher Love, *The Ministry of Angels* (London, 1657), p. 7; and, more important than any, St. Augustine in his commentary on Psalms.

78. Matthew Poole, *Annotations upon the Holy Bible* (London, 1688), on Psalm civ. See also H. Hammond, *A Paraphrase and Annotations upon the Book of the Psalms* (London?, ca. 1650).

as Professor W. C. Curry thinks,[79] a dichotomy of some sort.
Can it be that Milton followed Henry More's doctrine that
the angel is a spirit equivalent to the human soul except that
it informs an ethereal or aerial body instead of a terrestrial
one? Nothing explicitly said about angels in either *Paradise
Lost* or *Christian Doctrine* prevents this interpretation, but
Milton's whole conception of the human soul taken with the
evident parallel he intends in *Paradise Lost* between soul
and angel would seem to be against it. Miss Nicolson, quot-
ing Raphael on how a purified Adam may ascend ethereal
as angels, says that Milton and More both held man and
angel to differ in degree rather than in kind, and she is undoubtedly correct.[80] But since Milton and More disagreed
radically about the soul, the probability is that they disagreed also on the angel. More's cherished conviction of
pre-existence supports his contention that man dies into an
angel-like condition, putting off a terrestrial vehicle and putting on an aerial one, and it is supported by that contention;
but it is totally incompatible with Milton's equally cherished
conviction that "the whole man is soul" and is born and dies
as one. More himself makes the point that psychopannychites
deny vehicles.[81]

In *Paradise Lost,* it is true, Raphael once speaks of "every
Soule in Heav'n" (V.816) and again of "heav'nly Soules"
(VI.165); but nothing in the context suggests that he uses
these expressions in the sense that More applies the word
soul to all finite spirits "because they do vitally actuate the
Matter, be it *Aethereal, Aereal,* or *Terrestrial.*"[82] Raphael
seems rather by a common turn of speech to mean simply
"angel." If we should interpret him strictly and put on his
word *Soule* a meaning parallel to that which Milton in

79. Curry, p. 176.
80. Nicolson, p. 437.
81. Preface to *The Immortality of the Soul* (London, 1659).
82. *The Grand Mystery of Godliness* (London, 1660), II.iii.34.

Christian Doctrine gives it for man, we would suppose that an angel, like a man, is "a living being, intrinsically and properly one and individual, not compound or separable, not . . . made up and framed of two distinct and different natures."[83]

Most Platonist angelologists of the seventeenth century resembled More in their notion of dichotomy, but the occultist Robert Fludd had his own scheme. Fludd started with the old notion that whereas God is *Identity*, all creatures are *alterity*, that is, composed of an *internal* and an *external*. The angel's external is of the "Catholic Waters" which God divided as his first act of creation. It is the *hyle* or original matter which God had prepared to receive forms and which differentiates his infused "breath" or "light" into individual forms, varying in tenuity as they have more or less of the divine infusion. The angel's "internal," as it were the angel's soul,[84] is God's "light" or "breath," a part of his essence. Fludd calls it the "increate spirit" and the externum the "create spirit."[85]

This is a very different doctrine from More's, for plainly to Fludd an angel has no individual identity except as an existing combination of internal and external, whereas for More an angel's identity, like a man's, rests wholly in its "soul." Thus Fludd's angels are in a sense unitary beings; their dichotomy is that of potency and act, a division that even the Scholastics admit to angels, since only God can be pure act. [86]

Fludd, then, on composition in angels seems closer than

83. I.vii, *Works*, XIV, 41.

84. Fludd, *Answer* III.vi.50.

85. Fludd sketches his angelology in various places throughout *Mosaicall Philosophy*, in several early chapters of *Utriusque cosmi historia*, in the answer to Foster, and, most fully, in *Philosophia sacra* (Frankfurt, 1626) I, IV, II, I, II.i.207 ff. By courtesy of the Houghton Library at Harvard I have examined, though I cannot claim to have read, all Fludd's works.

86. *Summa theologica*, Q. 50, Art. II; Maldonat III.iv.31.

More to Milton. But like More, Fludd is at odds with Milton
on the nature of the human soul. Whereas Milton is tra-
ducian and mortalist, Fludd is neither; and whereas Milton
expressly denies that the life God breathed into man is of
the essence of God, Fludd affirms that the breath of God in
both soul and angel is of God's essence.[87] Milton may have
thought, like Fludd, that the angel had an internal inspired
by God and an external of some kind of matter, but he
could hardly have thought, like Fludd, that the internal was
the superior and virtuous part of the combination, for to
Milton "Matter, like the form and nature of the angels itself,
proceeded incorruptible from God."[88] Rather Milton would
have thought the angel's internal, like the spirit of man,
merely "an inspiration of some divine virtue fitted for the
exercise of life and reason. . . ."[89] The angel would be dichotomous, then, only in analysis, just as Milton distinguishes in
thought the spirit from the body—the latter considered as a
"mere senseless stock"; the infused part has no autonomy.
The spirit of man, Milton says, can never be supposed "separate from the body so as to have a perfect and intelligent
existence independent of it."[90] Neither, perhaps, for him
could the angelic spirit exist separate from its substance,
the ether.

So, in *Christian Doctrine* Milton very probably does not
mean dichotomy when he says that angels are "spirits . . .
and of ethereal nature." He may intend that, like man, they
are total beings, though more tenuous than man. Perhaps
he does not distinguish *spirit* from *ether* in More's way, by
establishing the Cartesian gulf between them, but distinguishes them as genus and species, ether being a kind of
spirit, a quasi-material substance of which angels and the

87. *Mosaical Philosophy* I, II.ii.15, 16; I, V.i.91; II, I.iv.149; etc.
88. *Christian Doctrine* I.vii, *Works*, XIV, 23.
89. *Ibid.* I.vii, *Works*, XIV, 41.
90. *Ibid.* I.vii, *Works*, XIV, 41, 43.

heavens are made. And thus, as I have argued above, in
Paradise Lost (V.496-498) he equates spirit with ether in
something like the Calvinist sense, referring to "the form
and nature of the angels" as one thing—"forma et natura ipsa
Angelorum."[91]

This usage would seem to accommodate the nebulous Calvinist idea of angels as unitary beings of rarefied body. The
Calvinists did not, of course, agree with Milton on the nature
of the soul any better than Fludd and More did. But they
did not contend for the same parallels between man and
angel that Fludd and More did. Whereas More held both
man and angel to be composed of soul and body, and Fludd
held the human soul itself to be "alterity," like the angel,[92]
the Calvinists held man to be soul and body, but the angel
only one—a kind of matter, apparently, with some properties
of soul. Milton thought man to be one—"the whole man is
soul, and the soul man." Perhaps then, in his view, the whole
angel is "soul" and the "soul" angel, a creature parallel to
man in a higher, more subtile being of the same kind.

VII

Though Milton may perhaps have renounced the Platonists' idea that angels had vehicles, he could not do without
some of their ideas on the details of angelic operation. In
this he was one with the Calvinist theologians, who deplored
the Platonist elaborations but who nevertheless had occasionally to resort to them. The Platonics, says Méric Casaubon, know more about spirits than anyone, and no wonder
since they have most studied spirits and with unlawful rites,

91. *Ibid.* I.vii, *Works,* XIV, 23.
92. Fludd, *Utriusque* I, IV.xi.123.

too; their souls are endangered, but what they say agrees with daily experience.[93]

Milton's principal levy on the Platonists was for the idea that angels can at will expand and contract their tenuous bodies. Of all his borrowing from Psellus this was the most serviceable to him, particularly as enabling one or two striking effects, such as Satan's towering up against the angelic guard. But it also led to the detailed inconsistencies first pointed out by Dr. Johnson and recently made much of by Mr. Waldock.[94] Johnson thought inconsistent such items as Satan's ability to take his spear with him into a toad and the good angels' inability to contract their armor to avoid cannon balls. Masson notes further that the devils apparently did contract their armor to crowd into Pandemonium. Mr. Waldock remarks that though an angel's substance is liquid, Moloch proclaims he will bind Gabriel and "drag him at his chariot wheels." "When all is said," thinks Mr. Waldock, "this is treating us very nearly as morons."

Perhaps if Milton had thought it worth while he could have removed these difficulties by being a little more specific. Suppose the devils stacked arms before entering Pandemonium? Suppose Moloch's words are just battlefield hyperbole? And note that Satan was "squat *like* a toad," not *in* a toad. These explanations are, perhaps, as sound as the complaints; no more literal-minded and just one step more speculative. But they hardly seem worth our trouble. Con-

---

93. See p. 43 of Casaubon's Preface to *A True and Faithful Relation of What Passed for Many Yeers between Dr. John Dee and Some Spirits* (London, 1659). Zanchy and others report Platonist ideas, sometimes in detail, but with reserve.

94. See Johnson's life of Milton and Waldock, pp. 109 ff. The nearest thing to an angelologist who has complained of *PL* in anything like Johnson's terms is Sir Samuel Morland in *The Urim of Conscience* (London, 1695), I.13 ff. Garnett says that Morland began the criticism of the materiality of the angels. Actually, however, Sir Samuel's criticism was not of materiality but of circumstantiality. He was merely making a conventional Calvinist complaint against a too curious knowledge of angels.

cede that Milton did not make his picture of angels and their equipment wholly free of detailed inconsistencies. His confusions, however, are not the result of a foolishly divided concept of celestial conditions, as Mr. Waldock supposes, but simply of occasional oversight or perhaps a dismissal of details almost too trivial to bother about. The difficulty about the armor does not rise insuperable out of a stupid effort to combine a "Homeric" picturization with a "Wellsian" idea of angelic substance, but simply out of a little carelessness or highhandedness in some of the details of the combination. The inconsistencies are surely too slight to matter much.[95]

Mr. Waldock says that Milton's notion of an angel's physical attributes was really rather nonsensical and that if Milton thought it "scientific" so much the worse for him. "Seventeenth-century science can do better than this." The fact is, though, that seventeenth-century pneumatological science could not do a bit better. The pneumatological theory was not, of course, evolved with literary use in mind; in details it was bound to fail Milton occasionally, and he even more certain to modify it. But in general he accepted the article on angelic expansion and contraction about as he found it. And he had almost of necessity to use either it or the scholastic rationale if he intended to establish his story as "scientific didacticism." Whether or not the pneumatological authorities were worthy of the respect which Mr. Waldock reproves Mr. Lewis for granting, they were the authorities recognized in Milton's time, and he had to follow them if he followed any.

Now I conclude thus [says Fludd]: If the externall substance

95. Theoretical angelology has little or nothing to say about arms or armor or any of the rest of angels' battle outfit, so that whatever Milton propounded of the special properties of this supernal equipment had of necessity to be outside that "science" which, as Mr. Lewis contends, Milton genuinely rested on for much.

of the Angel be ayre . . . then we know by the rules of Philosophy, that ayre subtiliated is fire, and againe ayre inspissated is a vapour, a mist, a cloud, and so by inspissation, ayre inuisible becommeth a visible substance . . . which being granted, what should hinder spirits, by contraction of this their external substances, to appeare when they please visibly, and organically to talke with a person, as the tempting spirit did to Christ? and againe, by an immediate dilatation of the same external aery spirit, to become inuisible, no otherwise then a smoake by dilatation vanisheth. . . .[96]

Millions of spiritual creatures walk the earth unseen to Adam and Eve, but the spiritual creatures named Raphael and Michael show themselves at will. Before the fall, Raphael's brightness is welcome and glorious; after it, Adam and Eve cannot sustain the pure angelic light, and Michael appears soberly in the likeness of a man. When the question was of angel visible to angel, the substance was the same proper substance that Adam and Eve saw, but the shape and the degree of rarefaction were different.

Well, then, when Satan swelled against the angelic guards, did he grow less visible to them? And if not, how but by such "dilatation" did he make himself invisible to his devils in Pandemonium when he returned there? The most reasonable answer is that though Milton wanted a show of "science" in these passages, he was not really trying to write angelology.

In two other passages, however—that on how angels profit by earthly food and that on how they make love with each other—Milton was perhaps trying to write angelology or something closely akin to it. I have explained in another

---

96. Fludd, *Answer* III.vi.51, 52. See also *Philosophia sacra*, p. 216. As Professor Hughes notes on *PL* V.415, Fludd's notion of the elements passing into each other is a Renaissance commonplace. See, for instance, "The Argument of the Front and of the Worke" in George Hakewill's *Apologie* (London, 1620).

and detailed discussion that as angelology these passages
are radically independent, are in fact almost completely
divorced from received angelological opinion. No authority
known to me allows that angel copulates with angel, and
only Fludd allows that angels can assimilate earthly food.[97]
This very independence would seem to argue Milton's zeal,
but as I have said above Milton is boldly adapting his picture of angels to suit his conviction (to which *Christian Doctrine* shows his strong attachment) that matter is good and
universal in creation. His zeal is genuine, but it is for his
general materialism rather than for angelology itself. Milton
is probably not following Fludd on the eating; but he is
strikingly like Fludd, who also used the point of angelology
casually to back a wider doctrine that interested him.

VIII

If the case I have argued is good, then in *Paradise Lost*
Milton has rejected the Scholastics on both substance and
apparition as a matter of both doctrine and literary convenience, and has rejected the Calvinists on apparition largely
as a matter of literary convenience. As a matter of piety he
has written on angels in the same spirit of devout humility
that the Calvinists adopted, and he has at least partly paralleled the somewhat compromised Calvinist doctrine that the
angelic essence is of the empyrean. As a matter of literary
opportunism he has used the Platonist doctrine of fluidity
and contractibility, but has perhaps rejected the key Platonist doctrine of angelic dichotomy. Finally, he has fitted his
idea of angelic substance into a more general idea of the scale
of nature, and by asserting that angels may assimilate human
food he has gone to the extreme of almost identifying human
and angelic substance.

97. Fludd, *Answer* III.vi.44.

It would seem, then, that in his angelology Milton was less widely eclectic than has sometimes been thought, and much more consistent, and once, at least, very independent. This could be taken to signify a greater respect for angelology as a "science" than some critics have supposed he had. But on the other hand, Milton has let his fiction control his angelology noticeably; and the very heart of his angelology is dominated and perhaps warped by his opinions on a question that transcended angelology.

One thing is sure: in his solution of the literary problem of portraying angels Milton did not rely merely on his own invention nor yet on a careless borrowing from patristic and medieval authorities; he made a rather painstaking synthesis of contemporary thought (which amply used the older writers) with his own bold ideas.

This is not an altogether new conclusion, but I have given it, I hope, some new backing.

ALLAN H. GILBERT

Milton's Defense of Bawdry

A S A STUDENT AT CAMBRIDGE, Milton took part in some of the learnedly comic exercises of the place. For one of them he wrote the following defense of comic license:

Let us free ourselves from the laws of oratory and plunge into comic license. If in this I should depart from my custom and from the strict laws of modesty by a finger's breadth, as they say, remember, fellow students, that I have stripped off and laid aside my old custom for your sake. Or if anything is spoken freely, or anything licentiously, you should conclude that it was suggested to me not by my spirit and nature but by the occasion of the time and the nature of the place.[1]

In this oration there is nothing more immodest than a scatological joke, such as perhaps his auditors would have been unprepared for from the Lady, even if it were known that he admired Erasmus' *Praise of Folly*.[2]

Milton next had occasion to discuss laughter in the preface of his *Animadversions on the Remonstrant's Defence*. He writes:

1. *Prolusion VI, The Works of John Milton*, ed. F. A. Patterson *et al.*, Columbia edition (New York, 1931-1938), XII, 226—hereafter cited as *Works*.
2. Milton may have written this in the spirit of Erasmus' *Moriae encomium*, which he praises as "ingeniosissimum, ... non infimi Scriptoris opus" (*Prolusion VI, Exercitationes nonnunquam Ludicras Philosophiae studiis non obesse, Works*, XII, 220). Erasmus represents Folly as saying on her relation to procreation:

Although in the serious uncasing of a grand imposture (for to deale plainly with you, Readers, Prelatry is no better) there be mixt here and there such a grim laughter, as may appeare at the same time in an austere visage, it cannot be taxt of levity or insolence: for even this veine of laughing (as I could produce out of grave Authors) hath oft-times a strong and sinewy force in teaching and confuting; nor can there be a more proper object of indignation and scorne together then a false Prophet taken in the greatest dearest and most dangerous cheat, the cheat of soules: in the disclosing whereof if it be harmfull to be angry, and withall to cast a lowring smile, when the properest object calls for both, it will be long enough ere any be able to say why those two most rationall faculties of humane intellect anger and laughter were first seated in the brest of man.[3]

Milton's adversary found in the "veine of laughing" of this tract some scatological passages to object to, as that on the princes who, wandering in the city streets by night to learn what their people are doing and saying, are obliged to lower their dignity enough "to accept quietly as a perfume, the over-head emptying of some salt lotion."[4] This to the opponent showed familiarity with playhouse and bordello. He objected also to a passage on the bishop's foot

---

Principio quid esse potest vita ipsa vel dulcius, vel pretiosius? At huius exordium cui tandem acceptum ferri convenit, nisi mihi [i.e., Moriae]? . . . Verum ipse Deûm pater atque hominum Rex, qui totum nutu tremefactat Olympum, fulmen illud trisulcum ponat oportet, & vultum illum Titanicum, quo, cum lubet, Deos omneis territat, planeque histrionum more, aliena sumenda misero persona, si quando velit id facere, quod numquam non facit, hoc est παιδοποιεῖν. Iam vero Stoici se Diis proximos autumant. At date mihi terque quaterque, aut si libet, sexcenties Stoicum, tamen huic quoque, si non barba insigne sapientiae, etiam si cum hircis commune, certe supercilium erit ponendum, explicanda frons, abjicienda dogmata illa adamantina, ineptiendum ac delirandum aliquantisper. In summa, me, me inquam, sapiens accersat oportet, si modo pater esse velit (*Moriae encomium,* in *Opera Amnia* [Lugduni Batavorum, 1703], IV, pp. 411-412).

3. *Animadversions, Works,* III, 107-108.
4. *Works,* III, 113; *Apology, Works,* III, 299.

which Milton, following Donne and Shakespeare, develops
into a joke on the "bad smell" of the bishop's socks.[5] Milton
vigorously defends his language, pointing out that "Christ
himselfe speaking of unsavory traditions, scruples not to
name the Dunghill and the Jakes." And further:

... the Spirit of God who is purity it selfe, when he would
reprove any fault severely, or but relate things done or said
with indignation by others, abstains not from some words
not civill at other times to be spok'n. Omitting that place in
Numbers at the killing of *Zimri and Cosbi* done by *Phineas*
in the heigth of zeal, related as the Rabbines expound, not
without an obscene word, we may finde in Deuteronomy
and three of the Prophets, where God denouncing bitterly
the punishments of Idolaters, tels them in a terme immodest
to be utter'd in coole blood, that their wives shall be defil'd
openly. But these, they will say were honest words in that
age when they were spok'n. Which is more then any Rabbin
can prove, and certainly had God been so minded, he could
have pickt such words, as should never have come into
abuse. What will they say to this. *David* going against *Nabal*,
in the very same breath when he had but just before nam'd
the *name of God*, he vowes not *to leave any alive of Nabals
house that pisseth against the wall.* But this was unadvisedly
spoke, you will answer, and set downe to aggravate his infirmity. Turne then to the first of Kings where God himselfe
uses the phrase; *I will cut off from Jereboam him that pisseth
against the wall.* Which had it beene an unseemely speech
in the heat of an earnest expression, then we must conclude
that *Jonathan, or Onkelos the Targumists* were of cleaner
language then he that made the tongue; for they render it
as briefly, *I will cut off all who are at yeares of discretion,*
that is to say so much discretion as to hide nakednesse.
Whereas God who is the author both of purity and elo-
quence, chose this phrase as fittest in that vehement character wherein he spake. Otherwise that plaine word might

5. *Apology*, introd., *Works*, III, 308.

have easily bin forborne. Which the *Masoreths* and Rab-
binicall *Scholiasts* not well attending, . . . gave us this insuls
rule out of their *Talmud, That all words which in the Law
are writ obscenely, must be chang'd to more civill words.*
Fools who would teach men to read more decently then
God thought good to write. And thus I take it to be manifest, that indignation against men and their actions notori-
ously bad, hath leave and autority oft times to utter such
words and phrases as in common talke were not so mannerly
to use. That ye may know . . . that all words and whatsoever
may be spoken shall at some time in an unwonted manner
wait upon [the] purposes [of virtue].[6]

Continuing, he shows the application of this to comedy:

Now that the confutant may also know as he desires, what
force of teaching there is sometimes in laughter, I shall returne him in short, that laughter being one way of answering
A Foole according to his folly, teaches two sorts of persons,
first the Foole himselfe *not to be wise in his own conceit;*
as *Salomon* affirms, which is certainely a great document, to
make an unwise man know himselfe. Next, it teaches the
hearers, in as much as scorne is one of those punishments
which belong to men carnally wise, which is oft in Scripture
declar'd; for when such are punisht *the simple are thereby
made wise,* if *Salomons* rule be true. And I would ask, to
what end *Eliah* mockt the false Prophets? was it to shew his
wit, or to fulfill his humour? doubtlesse we cannot imagine
that great servant of God had any other end in all which
he there did, but to teach and instruct the poore misledde
people. And we may frequently reade, that many of the
Martyrs in the midst of their troubles, were not sparing to
deride and scoffe their superstitious persecutors. Now may
the confutant advise againe with Sir *Francis Bacon* whether
Eliah and the Martyrs did well to turne religion into a
Comedy, or Satir; *to rip up the wounds* of Idolatry and
Superstition *with a laughing countenance.* So that for pious

6. *Apology,* sect. 1, *Works,* III, 315-317.

gravity his author here is matcht and overmatcht, and for wit and morality in one that followes.

> *—laughing to teach the truth*
> *What hinders? as some teachers give to Boyes*
> *Junkets and knacks, that they may learne apace.*

Thus *Flaccus* in his first Satir, and in his tenth

> *—Jesting decides great things*
> *Stronglier, and better oft then earnest can.*

I could urge the same out of *Cicero*, and *Seneca*, but he may content him with this. And hence forward, if he can learn, may know as well what are the bounds, and objects of laughter and vehement reproofe, as he hath knowne hitherto how to deserve them both. . . . So that the question ere while mov'd who he is that spends thus the benevolence of laughter and reproofe so liberally upon such men as the Prelats, may returne with a more just demand, who he is not of place and knowledge never so mean, under whose contempt and jerk these men are not deservedly falne?[7]

This theory of "plain" or "obscene" words in comedy directed against proper objects of reproof is still later exemplified. Milton's *Second Defence* is directed against Alexander More, a defender of King Charles. More had laid himself open to attack by amours with servant-girls, fit to be narrated, Milton says, as Milesian or Baian tales. Of one of them he writes jocosely:

The neighbors often noticed Morus alone with this girl going into a certain pergola in the garden. This is far from adultery, you say. And indeed it could be something or other else. Perhaps he was going to give some lecture to the girl who already had a little knowledge, and wanted to hear more discussion of gardens, those of Alcinous or Adonis for instance. He could have done no more than praise the flower-

7. *Ibid.*, 317-319.

beds or merely wish for shade; then, too, he could have shown the woman the method of grafting, that is, the way of inserting a mulberry into a fig, from which very soon sycamores would spring up, making a most pleasant walk. Who can deny that it may have been these and many other things?[8]

The mulberry was More, or Morus, himself, and the fig is from the Italian word *fica*, signifying the female genitals. On a very small scale Milton is doing something of what the Italian burlesque poets did. Molza, for example, wrote a poem called the *Ficheide*, or *Figead*, which Milton in his promiscuous reading probably had perused. At least, it appears that he could have obtained the word *fica* only from the Italian, where its associations are usually comic.

There is at least one instance of Milton's knowledge of Italian poetry depending largely on sexual double meanings for its comedy. Writing to Carlo Dati on April 21, 1647, he sends his salutations to the Gaddian Academy, naming several of its members, among them Malatesta, evidently Antonio Malatesti, author of *La Tina*. There is a persistent tradition that Malatesti presented to Milton a manuscript of this work; its title page runs thus: *La Tina, Equivoci rusticali in cinquanta sonetti di Antonio Malatesti, Fiorentino. Composti nella sua villa di Tajano il settembre dell'anno 1637 e da lui regalati al grande poeta inghilese Giovanni Milton. Londra, a spese dell'editore.*[9] The *equivoci* consist of plays on words such as Milton uses in attacking More. Parallels are as follows:

---

8. *Defensio secunda, Works,* VIII, 32. I have followed what seems the demand of the sense by shifting the position of one clause, without textual warrant.

9. Taken from the edition of Rome, 1946 (Nuova Biblioteca di Opere Lettararie Inedite o Rare), which follows the earlier edition of uncertain date. See J. Milton French, *The Life Records of John Milton* (New Brunswick, 1949), I, 375, and his references.

La Tina		Milton
1.14	*la coda*	*Pro se def.* 116.7
18.14	*coda*	
2.	*stile*	*2 def.* 142.9, 10, 13
7.1	*fico*	*2 def.* 32.8
25.14	*fico*	*Pro se def.* 94.15, 108.12, 136.4
45.title	*innestare*	*2 def.* 32.8, 10^{10}

It appears, quite contrary to the suggestions of Masson and others, that Milton found something to interest him in *La Tina*, and that he applied it in ridiculing More.

In further ridicule, Milton praises the clever brain of the man who composed on another amour of Morus the distich that may be rendered thus:

> *Since Pontia is with child from lying with you, More,*
> *Who can deny that she is properly moralled and full of*
> morality?[11]

The comedy of bawdy double meaning also appears in these passages:

I wrote these words on the edition, long expected, of that noble book; but while, as you say, Salmasius was laboring on its impression [i.e., printing], you were disgracing his house by a shameful compression of Pontia.[12]

So you say in a threatening tone: "Sometime, you nasty beasts, you shall find out what pencils can do." Shall we find you out, you chaser of servant-maids, you whore-master, or your pencil, which is to be feared only by servant-maids? If anybody should just show you a radish or a mullet, by Hercules, you would think you had got off easily, if you were

---

10. Cf. Rabelais, *Pantagruel* III.xix.
11. *Defensio secunda, Works,* VIII, 36.
12. *Ibid.,* 56.

able to escape without having your rump slit, and with that obscene pencil [i.e., penis] of yours safe.[13]

But far from endeavoring to palliate More's charge that he had written obscenely, Milton expressed regret only for his moderation:

... But now I come to that which offended More—the most holy and by far the most chaste man of his age—to wit, that I use filthy speech,[14] words obscene and of double-meaning. What a wretched and prostitute creature! You to rebuke filthy words who do not blush in doing the basest deeds! Indeed I would not repent now if I had used words of that sort a little more freely, if I should gain nothing more from it than bringing out from you this most dishonest pretense, or through it tearing off your mask and showing you plainly to everybody as the vilest of hypocrites. For what that is said in my whole book, what word, is more filthy than this word *More?* For not in word nor in matter, but in you is every vice and complete obscenity. You, baser than any faun or obscene satyr, have made good words obscene by your morals. No shade, not even that fig-tree, could conceal your baseness. He who speaks of you and your scapes has to use bawdy language.

And so if to your reproach I have used obscene words, I can easily defend myself by the example of the greatest authors, who have always believed that plain and homely words when delivered with indignation do not show obscenity but the vigor of the sternest rebuke. Who ever made

13. *Ibid.*, 142. See also VIII, 34, 17-19; 38, 2-3; 46, 2, 8, 15; 88, 8-11; 92, 10-11; 110, 13-14; 114, 19—116, 3; 142, 20; 168, 6; 184, 1, 7-8; *Pro se defensio*, Works, IX, 52, 2, 8-10; 54, 5-6; 62, 20-21; 66, 15-17; 94, 12—96, 2; 116, 7-8, 20—122, 11; 128, 16-17; 134, 19—136, 5; 142, 2-4, 20-21; 188, 13-14; 190, 7; 202, 7-8; 206, 21—208, 2; 252, 13-14; 270, 7-9, 17-19; 280, 17-19; 284, 14-20.

For the *cauda* of p. 116, cf. Horace *Satires* I.ii.45; II.vii.49; and Charles S. Singleton, *Nuovi canti carnascialeschi del Rinascimento* (Modena, 1940), p. 143, *s.v. coda.* With Milton's play on *pencil*, cf. Aldous Huxley, *Eyeless in Gaza*, ch. 30, end.

14. *Illotus*, Jonson's *unwashed*, applied to bawdry *(Volpone*, dedication).

it a fault in Piso, the writer of the *Annals*,[15] who because of
his goodness and his chaste habits was called Frugi, that in
those *Annals* he complained that "the young men were
devoted to the prick?" Who ever censured Sallust, a most
weighty writer, because in his *History* he actually says: "By
belly, by hand, by prick, by dice, by inherited wealth, Rome
is torn in pieces." Do I need to mention Herodotus, Seneca,
Suetonius,[16] Plutarch,[17] the mosty weighty of authors? If you
deny that they sometimes use words even more than unchaste and mix the basest things with more serious matters,
you announce that you are not versed in those authors. If
this is improper in every time and place, how often would
you have to write an accusation of obscenity against the
most learned Erasmus,[18] who stands up in bronze at Rotter-
dam, how often against our Thomas More,[19] whose name
you disgrace with yours, how often, too, against the fathers
of the Church themselves—Clement of Alexandria,[20] Arno-
bius,[21] Lactantius,[22] Eusebius—while they unveil or mock
the obscene mysteries of the ancient religions! . . . You call
on Marcus Tullius in vain; for if he in that golden book
De officiis,[23] which you cite, says that jesting of that type
is in good taste, witty, clever, and pleasing—and to that type
is to be assigned not merely Plautus and the ancient comedy

15. The note in the Columbia edition suggests that Milton took this
reference to Piso, and the Greek word in 110, 21, from Cicero *Fam.* IX.22.
   Randolph also makes use of this letter in *The Muses' Looking-glass* IV.ii
(*Poetical and Dramatic Works of Thomas Randolph*, ed. W. Carew Hazlitt
[London, 1875], I, 244-245).
16. Cf. Sir John Harington, *Metamorphosis of Ajax*, ed. Peter Warlock
and Jack Lindsay (London, 1927), sect. 1, p. 43.
17. Harington (p. 33) refers to Plutarch *Symposeons* V.i.
18. Perhaps a reference to Erasmus' *Colloquies*, for example *Uxor*
Μεμψίγαμος.
19. Cf. Harington, sect. 1, pp. 38-39, 44.
20. *Protrepticus pros Hellenas* II.x.39, ed. Otto Stahlin, in *Die griechischen
christlichen Schriftsteller der ersten drei Jahrhunderte* (Leipzig, 1936),
I.11-29.
21. *Adversus gentes*, Book 4, chs. 7, 19, 20, 21, etc., in *Patrologiae cursus
completus*, ed. J. P. Migne (Paris, 1844), V, 1003 ff.
22. Cf. Harington, p. 30.
23. *De officiis* 1.104.

of the Athenians, but also the books of the Socratic philosophers, as you might read there—, he does not seem to me to
have set limits so much too narrow, so much too strict, that
it would be hard for anybody to keep within them,—certainly
not such that I do not keep within them.[24]

In his authorities Milton is partially in agreement with Sir
John Harington, whose defense of plain speaking in his
Metamorphosis of Ajax may be compared with Milton's. The
example of Saint Thomas More is especially illuminating.
That saint composed a comic epigram on the knight who
found difficulty in kissing a lady with a long nose, and applied a bawdy *a fortiori* argument in the epigram on a girl
riding horseback astride.[25]
    Milton's final rejoinder is the following:

As to those jests that you say, falsely, were taken from the
bawdy-house and the tavern (unless by taken from the
bawdy-houses you mean to say that they dragged out you
who were hiding there), if all other men admit that they
are not undignified and not ignoble but dignified and witty
and allowed as salt to be rubbed on your rottenness, then
indeed that stupid professor's ignorance of yours is evident
enough here, as in so many other places, when you say that
such jesting is indecorous.[26]

So Milton holds that an obscene subject may properly be
dealt with in obscene terms by the most honorable and
modest men. Indeed, he asserts that it is not "out-of-the-way
and immodest for an author in the same book both to assail
baseness with sharpness and wit ... and also to think about
God."[27] Likewise, Milton will not allow that his familiarity

    24. *Pro se defensio, Works,* IX, 106-112.
    25. *In puellam divaricatis tibiis equitantem.*
    26. *Pro se defensio, Works,* IX, 174. See also 80, 96, 122, 180-182, 189,
200.
    27. *Works,* pp. 180-182.

with bawdy language implies anything ignoble in his personal conduct. This is to approve the poet Herrick's assertion of himself at the end of *Hesperides:*

> *Jocond his Muse was; but his Life was chast.*[28]

Milton's verse offers only hints of the comedy of sex. He does, however, give one statement in verse of the folly associated with love and sex that carries further his theory of comedy. Adam in his conversation with the angel has indulged in more than temperate praise of Eve, which marks him as the enthusiastic lover so carried away by his passion as to approach the verge of comedy. The angel vigorously corrects his enthusiasm, substituting a less extravagant love:

> *that with honour thou maist love*
> *Thy mate, who sees when thou art seen least wise.*[29]

Raphael has in mind the effect of love in causing man to turn to folly, to make himself a subject for comedy. He seems especially to have in mind sexual intercourse, often represented as foolish; for example, Sir Thomas Browne, with Montaigne in mind, remarked:

I could be content that we might procreate like trees, without conjunction, or that there were any way to perpetuate the World without this trivial and vulgar way of coition; it is the foolishest act a wise man commits in all his life; nor

---

28. Marino is less apologetic:

> Sia modesto l'Autor; che sien le carte
> Men pudiche talhor, curar non deve.
> (*L'Adone* VIII.6)

Both had in mind Martial's "Lasciva est nobis pagina, vita proba" (I.4), Catullus' XVI, "Nam castum esse decet pium poetam / Ipsum, versiculos nihil necesse est," and perhaps the verse written by the Emperor Hadrian, "Lasciuus uersu, mente pudicus eras" (Apuleius, *Apologia* XI, in *Opera*, ed. Rudolfus Helm [Lipsiae, 1905], II, 13).

29. *PL* VIII.577-578.

is there any thing that will more deject his cool'd imagination, when he shall consider what an odd and unworthy
piece of folly he hath committed.[30]

Herrick's putting of the tradition is briefer:

> *Not Jove*
> *Himselfe, at one time, can be wise, and Love.*[31]

Sir Thomas, unlike Herrick, is hardly touching lightly when
he indicates the folly associated with procreation, but Milton's passage, with the crestfallen Adam rebuked by the
angel, suggests the comic lover. And this in spite of Milton's
defense of the sanctity of sexual relations in an earlier passage;[32] yet even there he cannot refrain from referring to
the "bestial herds," with implication that man the lover easily
lapses toward them. When love conquers reason, the lover
is comic. Machiavelli is justified in making love one of the
prime sources of comic folly.[33]

And so there is an aura of comedy about a later instance
of the sexual relations of Adam and Eve, namely, that after
the fatal fruit has been taken. Intoxicated by it, Adam and
Eve in their folly

> *fansie that they feel*
> *Divinitie within them breeding wings*
> *Wherewith to scorn the Earth. . . .*[34]

But a comic quality appears in the contrasted reality; they
really feel only sexual excitement. Adam praises Eve as

---

30. *Religio Medici* II.ix, ed. Charles Sayle (Edinburgh, 1927), I, 100.
31. "To Silvia" ("Pardon my trepasse"). Montaigne cites "la parole
d'Agesilaus, que la prudence et l'amour ne peuvent ensemble" (*Essais* III.v,
ed. Pierre Villey [Paris, 1931], III, 217). Cf. III, 190, etc.
32. *PL* IV.741-743.
33. Prologue to *Clizia.*
34. *PL* IX.1009-1011.

sapient and judicious, qualities she has not been showing, and absurdly wishes ten trees had been forbidden instead of one. Adam shows an excessive eagerness and Eve is "nothing loath." The scene is a parody of the earlier one. In the first instance their intercourse is such as to drive adulterous lust from men to range among the bestial herds; here they burn in lust. The scene, even to the "shadie bank," suggests the jocose poems of other Restoration authors, such as "Under the Willow Shades" of the *Windsor Drollery*. To this association is added the stronger one of the sources Milton is imitating, the incidents of Paris and Helen in the third book of the *Iliad*, and of Zeus and Hera in the fourteenth.[35] Both are comic. Indeed, Homer comments on Zeus, deceived by the wiles of Hera, that "love and sexual desire and allurement snatch away the wits even of the wise."[36] Yet Milton always keeps the unmistakable comedy of the scene subdued and subordinate to his serious purpose; he even allows, though still keeping the contrast with the commendable scene in their bower before the Fall,[37] that their "love's disport" is "the solace of their sin." Had Milton held the ascetic belief that sexual intercourse was the sin of the Fall, he could hardly have touched this scene with comedy, but when he rejects that ascetic absurdity and makes this scene of "amorous play" only a pendant, without effect on the fate of those concerned, comic undertone becomes possible.

Even in *Paradise Regained* the comedy of sex is suggested. Belial advises that Jesus be tempted by setting women in his way, explaining that men tangled in amorous nets lose their strength and wisdom, are dissolved with voluptuous hope, and are drawn out with credulous desire; in short, they are made comic. Satan answers by belittling Belial:

35. Mentioned also in *PR* II.214-215.
36. *Iliad* XIV.216-217.
37. *PL* IV.741 ff.

> ... *because of old*
> *Thou thy self doat'st on womankind, admiring*
> *Thir shape, thir colour, and attractive grace,*
> *None are, thou think'st, but taken with such toys.*
> *Before the Flood thou with thy lusty Crew,*
> *False titl'd Sons of God, roaming the Earth*
> *Cast wanton eyes on the daughters of men,*
> *And coupl'd with them, and begot a race.*
> *Have we not seen, or by relation heard,*
> *In Courts and Regal Chambers how thou lurk'st,*
> *In Wood or Grove by mossie Fountain side,*
> *In Valley or Green Meadow to way-lay*
> *Some beauty rare,* Calisto, Clymene,
> Daphne, *or* Semele, Antiopa,
> *Or* Amymone, Syrinx, *many more*
> *Too long, then lay'st thy scapes on names ador'd....*[38]

The tone of Satan's speech is that of a superior whoremonger addressing an inferior one. The key is given by the word *scapes*,[39] adapted to jocose reference. The shepherd in *The Winter's Tale* says when he finds the infant Perdita: "Sure some scape: though I am not bookish, yet I can read waiting-gentlewoman in the scape. This has been some stair-work, some trunk-work, some behind-door-work; they were warmer that got this than the poor thing is here."[40]

---

38. *PR* II.174-189.
39. For *scapes,* see Nashe, *Foure Letters Confuted,* in *Works,* ed. Ronald B. McKerrow (London, 1904-1910), I, 286. Nashe's suggestion rests ultimately on Ovid's *Tristia* II.103-106, III.v.49-54. Jupiter says to Callisto in Warner's *Albion's England* (London, 1612):

> And there on beds, in bushes heere (My fainings fit so well)
> We may enjoy what love enjoyed, and none our scapes shall tell.
> (Bk. 2, ch. 11, p. 51)

Cf. also *Albion's England,* Bk. 7, ch. 36, p. 172; *NED;* and the note in Todd's edition of *Paradise Regained.*
40. *The Winter's Tale* III.iii.78-82.

A more obvious comic scene is furnished by *Samson Agonistes*. The Chorus, seeing Dalila approach, exclaims:

> *But who is this, what thing of Sea or Land?*
> *Female of sex it seems,*
> *That so bedeckt, ornate, and gay,*
> *Comes this way sailing*
> *Like a stately Ship*
> *Of* Tarsus, *bound for th' Isles*
> *Of* Javan *or* Gadier
> *With all her bravery on, and tackle trim,*
> *Sails fill'd, and streamers waving,*
> *Courted by all the winds that hold them play,*
> *An Amber sent of odorous perfume*
> *Her harbinger, a damsel train behind....*[41]

Dalila "overlai'd with wanton *tresses,* and in a flaring tire," and "bespecckl'd ... with all the gaudy allurements of a Whore"[42] is made comic in her comparison to the full-rigged ship such as Milton may have seen in *Lingua,* and which not many years before he composed *Samson* he himself had applied to the comic appearance of the clergy in their full costume:

... they would request us to indure still the russling of their Silken Cassocks, and that we would burst our *midriffes* rather then laugh to see them under Sayl in all their Lawn, and Sarcenet, their shrouds, and tackle, with a *geometricall rhomboides* upon their heads....[43]

In *Samson* Dalila is not, as in *PL* IX.1060, called a harlot; she is Samson's wife, but her temperament, with its lust, avarice, and infidelity, is whorish enough. Moreover, the

41. *SA* 710-721.
42. *Of Reformation, Works,* III, 25.
43. *Of Reformation, Works,* III, 74.

comparison of a woman with a ship, splendid though it is here, is generally derogatory and sexual. As such it links Dalila with the whores of the drama, who appear as less dignified ships, especially pinnaces. Ursula, the pig-woman of *Bartholomew Fair*, has been brought before Justice Overdo, "punk, pinnace, and bawd, any time these two and twenty years."[44] The "sumptuous" Dalila bears a serious part in the tragedy, but is incidentally comic as an over-dressed Philistine matron who has some kinship not only with the "lazar kite of Cressid's kind" but even with Doll Tearsheet.

Milton deals with the use of plain or bawdy language in two situations. The first is the instance of strong feeling, as when God denounced the wickedness of the Jews. The second is the comic employment of such language. The two uses are not altogether distinct, because comedy and other literature had for Milton a function primarily didactic. Such was the view usual in his age, stated by Sidney, Heywood, and others. Ben Jonson repeatedly insisted on the high function of the comic writer. Yet in the practice of the playwright, not every passage could be unmistakably didactic; some must serve to carry on the plot or even amuse the audience. They would be covered by Puttenham's words: "Yet

44. II.ii. The courtesans Λέμβιον καὶ Κερκούριον likened to boats in the *Greek Anthology* v.44. Cf. Plautus *Cassaria* V.iii.2766-2767; "A virgin pinnace, rigged and gay with all her flags" (Shirley, *Love's Cruelty* III.i, *The Dramatic Works and Poems of James Shirley*, ed. Alexander Dyce [London, 1833], II, 225). See also Shirley, *Coronation* III.ii in *Dramatic Works*, III, 499. Also Evelyn, *Tyrannus: or the Mode:* "A Fregat newly rigg'd kept not half such a clatter in a storme, as this Puppets streamers did when the wind was in his shrouds" (*Memoirs*, ed. William Bray [London, 1819], II, 313).

See also Fletcher, *Wit Without Money* I.i (*The Works of Beaumont and Fletcher*, ed. Arnold Glover and A. R. Waller [Cambridge, 1906], p. 153); Thomas Dekker, *Dekker His Dreame* in *The Non-Dramatic Works of Thomas Dekker*, ed. A. B. Grosart (London, 1885), III, 50, and *Lanthorne and Candlelight*, ibid., 269; Manningham's *Diary*, ed. John Bruce (Westminster, 1868), p. 12; *NED*.

will ye see in many cases how pleasant speeches and savour-
ing some skurrillity and unshamefastnes have now and then
a certaine decencie, and well become both the speaker to
say, and the hearer to abide." And he refers to "poems of
Homer, Ovid, Vergill, Catullus and other notable writers of
former ages, which were not of any gravitie or seriousness,
and many of them full of impudicitie and ribaudrie . . . and
yet those trifles are come from many former siecles unto our
times, uncontrolled or condemned or supprest by any Pope
or Patriarch or other severe censor of the civill maners of
men, but have bene in all ages permitted as the convenient
solaces and recreations of mans wit."[45] Milton's two poems
on Hobson the Carrier show him willing to indulge in literary
trifling, though they are quite without bawdry.

The comic authors Milton liked suggest what his practice
would have been had he attempted comedy. Aristophanes
he calls the "loosest" of the old comedians and a book "of
grossest infamy,"[46] yet he refers to the Greek as though not
unfamiliar with him, and annotators have traced to him
passages in *Paradise Regained*.[47] He had no objection to
the reading of "scurrill Plautus" and thought his jests, like
those of the old Greek comedians, "elegant, urbane, clever,
and witty."[48] The bawdry of Shakespeare and Jonson did
not cause Milton to withhold his admiration. The sexual
double meaning jocosely employed in the attack on More is
quite such as a comic author familiar with Italian literature
might employ.

Altogether, Milton's literary background, his theory of
what is allowable in stirring up laughter, and his practice
in both verse and prose—especially his treatment of More

45. *The Arte of English Poesie,* ed. Gladys Dodge Willcock and Alice
Walker (Cambridge, 1936), Bk. 2, ch. 9; Bk. 3, ch. 23.
46. *Areopagitica, Works,* IV, 299, 316.
47. Newton's notes on IV.244, 270.
48. *Areopagitica, Works,* IV, 307; *Pro se defensio, Works,* IX, 112.

—lead one to suppose that had he attempted comedy he would, when required by decorum—"the grand masterpiece to observe"[49]—not have hesitated to set down passages as bawdy as some of those in Jonson and Shakespeare, his favorite English comedians.

49. *Of Education, Works,* IV, 286.

R. H. BOWERS

The Accent on Youth in Comus

A conscientious artist responsible for the planning of Court functions was confronted by two problems: he had to give unity to a production in which music, poetry, painting, and dancing all played a part: he had to give beauty to a performance which was chiefly appreciated as an advertisement of wealth and an opportunity for flattery and political propaganda.

ENID WELSFORD[1]

———————

T HIS ESSAY PROPOSES A WAY—not *the* way—of reading Milton's masque that differs in emphasis from those hitherto accepted. I propose that it be read as a play concerned both directly and obliquely with the emotional life of youth, written by a youthful author largely for youthful performers, and for an aristocratic audience which both relished the spectacle of privileged youth and also felt therein some compulsive nostalgia for its own departed youth. In the critical literature of the past decade the text of *Comus* has been read or "used" in at least two other ways: as a document in Milton's artistic, intellectual, or moral development,[2] and as an "answer" to libertine doc-

1. *The Court Masque* (Cambridge, 1927), p. 247.
2. Cf. Arthur Barker, *Milton and the Puritan Dilemma: 1641-1660* (Toronto, 1942), pp. 9-16; J. C. Maxwell, "The Pseudo-Problem of Comus," *Cambridge Journal*, I (1948), 376-380; D. C. Allen, "Milton's *Comus* as a Failure in Artistic Compromise," *ELH*, XVI (1949), 104-119.

trines of the time.[3] Now, while such uses can certainly be rewarding when judiciously pursued, an implication is created that, after all, *Comus* is not great poetry, or that it did not do its job on the evening of September 29, 1634.

An obvious fact about John Milton's masque is that it was played before an upper-class audience at Ludlow Castle on September 29, 1634, as part of the inaugural festivities attendant on the assumption of the office of Lord President of Wales by the Earl of Bridgewater. The roles of the Lady, Elder Brother, and Younger Brother were taken by the earl's three children: the Lady Alice Egerton, Lord Brackley, and Mr. Thomas Egerton. As a play it "faced an audience" intimately; hence, its general import had to be readily intelligible and congenial. Possibly, as Mr. C. S. Lewis has argued,[4] the original acting version of the play was more "dramatic," less "literary," and less heavily moralized, than the revised 1637 text with which most readers are familiar. We can but conjecture about the staging of the entertainment,[5] our imaginations helped by the handsome illustrations in such basic works on the Stuart masque as Nicoll's *Stuart Masques and the Renaissance Stage* and Kernodle's *From Art to Theatre*. We can indulge in many conjectures; but the fundamental

3. G. F. Sensabaugh, "The *Milieu* of *Comus*," *SP*, XLI (1944), 238-249, argues that *Comus* is in part a Puritan "answer" to the specious Platonism of Henrietta Maria's circle that a "beautiful woman can do no wrong"; J. H. Hanford, *John Milton, Englishman* (New York, 1949), p. 63, suggests that *Comus* may have been written as a reply to the libertine philosophy embodied in Thomas Randolph's *The Muse's Looking Glass*.

4. "A Note on *Comus*," *RES*, VIII (1932), 170-176.

5. Hanford, p. 62, speculates that "the production would perhaps have striven to rival the royal pageantry of London in its magnificence, for the Lord President was actually a viceroy and his success in ruling the 'old and haughty nation' through his council of Welsh nobility depended on prestige." The enormous cost of maintaining country households was driving many hard-pressed country families into taking up permanent abodes in London; cf. F. J. Fisher, "The Development of London as a Centre of Conspicuous Consumption in the Sixteenth and Seventeenth Centuries," *Transactions of the Royal Historical Society*, 4th ser., XXX (1948), 37-50.

fact about *Comus* is that it was devised as an entertainment for an upper-class audience.

It has always been difficult to say much that was meaningful about the Renaissance concern with such literary forms as the pastoral, the masque, and the fanciful prose or verse romance[6] of damsels in distress and adolescent heroes on trial. Most of the literary historians have written in the now somewhat hackneyed terms of escape-literature, wish-fulfillment, nostalgia for Arcadia or the Golden Age, or urban yearning for the supposed peace and medicinal calm of a carefully manicured countryside. But insufficient stress has been placed on the direct concern of such art forms with the sensibilities and emotional experiences of the adolescent. These literary genres are not burdened by such bourgeois activities as trade or struggle for place, or by the desperate proletarian struggle for existence, or by the rude intrusion of strained logomachias freighted with political and theological ideology.[7] The subject matter hinges on such themes as love and loyalty, themes readily apprehended and relished by youth.[8]

The *donnée* of *Comus,* that of sensual temptation, deals with a situation as readily understood and felt by the adolescent as the themes of love and loyalty; in fact, they are often closely related. And the specific theme of seduction indignantly resisted by a spirited young lady who declaims vigorously thereafter on the virtue of chastity was commonplace on the Jacobean and Caroline professional stage. Professor R. S. Forsythe, in his study of the plays of James

6. Cf., in general, A. J. Tieje, *The Theory of Characterization in Prose Fiction Prior to 1740,* University of Minnesota Studies in Language and Literature, No. 5 (Minneapolis, 1916).

7. The pastoral, of course, played host at times to elements of ecclesiastical satire, as in *Lycidas,* or, better still, Quarles's *Shepherds' Oracles* (1646).

8. H. R. Patch, "Geoffrey Chaucer and Youth," *College English,* XI (Oct., 1949), 14-22, calls attention to Chaucer's recurrent concern with youthful characters and their problems.

Shirley, has noted that Shirley employed this theme in twelve separate plays, and that it occurred at least seventy-five times in the writings of other professional dramatists.[9] It was, accordingly, a congenial literary convention of the time, just as it was a social convention of the time that a girl of thirteen or fourteen had attained the status of womanhood. This later convention was painful in a theatrical temptation scene to some Victorian and Edwardian literary historians. For example, W. W. Greg wrote in 1906:

Milton has deliberately penned passages of smug conceit upon a subject whose delicacy he was apparently incapable of appreciating, and these passages he has placed, to be spoken in her own person, in the mouth of a child [Lady Alice Egerton was fifteen when she enacted the role of the Lady in *Comus*] just passing into the first dawn of adolescence, thereby outraging at once the innocence of childhood and the reticence of youth.[10]

However, numerous examples from the texts of the Elizabethan dramatists can be summoned to testify that thirteen or fourteen was considered an age of consent at that time. For example, in Jonson's *The Magnetic Lady* Compass refers to

> . . . *her niece, Mistress Placentia Steel,*
> *Who strikes the fire of full fourteen to-day,*
> *Ripe for a husband!*[11]

9. *The Relation of Shirley's Plays to the Elizabethan Drama* (New York, 1914), pp. 69-71. Professor Hermann Schaus has recently added Marlowe and Shakespeare to Spenser, Jonson, Fletcher, and Peele as writers whose works were echoed or paralleled in *Comus*: cf. his "The Relation of *Comus* to *Hero and Leander* and *Venus and Adonis*," *University of Texas Studies in English: 1945-1946* (Austin, 1946), pp. 129-141. The basic source study, however, is that of Ralph H. Singleton, "Milton's *Comus* and the *Comus* of Erycius Puteanus," *PMLA*, LVIII (1943), 949-957.

10. *Pastoral Poetry and Pastoral Drama* (London, 1906), p. 401.

11. *The Magnetic Lady* I.i.204-206.

Furthermore, in *Comus* we have a dispute conducted in the manner of youth, in the eristic manner of logomachia —the literal Lady is never really persuaded, never even slightly tempted, by the ingenious arguments of Comus; her first reaction to the sounds of revel is one of blue-stocking disgust:

> *I should be loath*
> *To meet the rudenesse, and swill'd insolence*
> *Of such late Wassailers.*[12]

Youth is literal-minded and dogmatic, unused to the devious accommodations of the sophisticate. Hence, as has often been noted, *Comus* is rather dramatized debate than the sort of genuine drama wherein the psychology of the tempter has penetrated, or is already shared by, the tempted, as in the marvelously mature temptation episodes between Satan and Eve in *Paradise Lost*.

The moral conflict is limned in black and white, which is the way unsubtle youth wants to regard the choices of life; the concern is with the immediate, the directly apprehended, rather than with the before and after, which is often the source of the adult's moral turmoil and anguish. The lurking dangers of the perilous woods are readily perceived and combated; after the unjust encounter youth is reassured by the happy outcome that this is a safe world, ultimately protected by the armed intervention of ever-watchful guardians. The danger was not really dangerous after all; this is the world of privileged children. There is a noticeable similarity in the tone and content of *Comus* to Ovid's *Metamorphoses*, whose world of myth and poetry Gilbert Murray has described as

a world of wonderful children where nobody is really cross

---

12. *Comus* 177-179.

or wicked except the grown-ups; Juno, for instance, and people's parents, and of course a certain number of Furies and Witches. . . . His criticism of life is very slight; it is the criticism passed by a child, playing alone and peopling the summer evening with delightful shapes, upon the stupid nurse who drags it off to bed. And that too is a criticism that deserves attention.[13]

There are other considerations which can be quickly tabulated to enforce this point of view about *Comus*. The language and versification, deliberately varied and perhaps experimental in some respects, is on the whole dignified, "dainty," and ceremonious; it is therefore language which would not bruise the tender sensibilities and sense of social propriety of youth. The Renaissance woof of recondite and classical allusion in the texture of the language is likewise appropriate to the cultural sensibilities of both audience and schoolboy actors; it also affords the youthful author means for thematic expansion and validation.

Finally, if one considers the performance of *Comus* in its social milieu, it can be argued that the high point of the entertainment was not when the Lady refused to partake of the enchanted cup (the audience knew that she wouldn't), but when the children of the Earl of Bridgewater were presented by the attendant Spirit, when they stepped out of character:[14]

> *Noble Lord, and Lady bright,*
> *I have brought ye new delight,*
> *Here behold so goodly grown*
> *Three fair branches of your own,*
> *Heav'n hath timely tri'd their youth,*
> *Their faith, their patience, and their truth.*

13. *Tradition and Progress* (Boston and New York, 1922), p. 117.
14. Enid Welsford (p. 318) argues that the "essential moment" of *Comus* is when the Lady refuses to drink from the enchanted cup.

And sent them here through hard assays
With a crown of deathless Praise,
To triumph in victorious dance
O're sensual Folly, and Intemperance.[15]

But perhaps the cliché "step out of character" is not quite
accurate—possibly they were never very far out of character
as far as the audience was concerned. For one of the peculiarities of the courtly entertainment is that the noble actor,
be he vocal or mute, is, in a real sense, also a spectator or
part of the audience to a greater degree than that characteristic of the professional actor in a public theatre. His importance derives mainly from his social position and his
integration with the social or political event which the
courtly entertainment was devised to celebrate—he is a "part
of the party." The primary social purpose of the masque is
this celebration of a political occasion; although in actual
performance the aesthetic and moral values of the masque
may temporarily fill the apprehension of both audience and
noble actors. Ben Jonson, of course, was always attempting
to enrich the masque with first-rate poetry; he never wanted
it to be a mere thing of "painting and carpentry."[16] Milton
was of a similar viewpoint, as evidenced by his moralistic
revision of the *Comus* text.[17]

The happy ending of youth triumphant over the gross
temptations of "sensual Folly, and Intemperance," then, pro-
vides a conventional, happy tone to a happy social gathering

15. *Comus* 966-975.
16. Cf. Ben Jonson, "An Expostulation with Inigo Jones," *Works*, ed.
W. Gifford (London, 1846), p. 658.
17. Hanford suggests (p. 62) that Henry Lawes, who produced *Comus*,
had to cut the literary weight of Milton's text in order to make it suitable
for social entertainment. The collaboration between Milton and Lawes, as
far as the available evidence permits, has been carefully studied by Willa
M. Evans in her *Henry Lawes: Musician and Friend of Poets* (New York,
1941), pp. 90-109.

in a great hall of the great. Throughout, the accent on youth has been tactfully maintained and enforced, in a happy poetic enterprise for young John Milton. Happy in that the subject matter enabled him to provide an appropriate libretto for a noble entertainment as well as an indirect outlet for his own restless struggling with some basic moral considerations characteristic of the "monkish rigor of Horton":

> *I thought, if I could draw my paines,*
> *Through Rimes vexation, I should them allay,*
> *Griefe brought to numbers cannot be so fierce,*
> *For, he tames it, that fetters it in verse.*[18]

18. John Donne, "The Triple Foole," *Poems*, ed. H. J. C. Grierson (Oxford, 1929), ll. 8-11.

ALWIN THALER

Shakespeare and Milton Once More

THIS STUDY SUPPLEMENTS two earlier essays of
mine on "The Shakespearean Element in Milton."
The first of these appeared in 1925,[1] and was then
revised and, with substantial additions, for some of which
I was indebted to the collections of other scholars, reprinted
in 1929 in my *Shakespeare's Silences*.[2] This later version of
the study examined approximately 250 passages in Milton's
work, early and late, which seemed significantly reminiscent
of Shakespeare—that is to say, of thirty-five of his plays. The
evidence indicated clearly what one would have expected:
that some of the great plays impressed Milton's memory far
more deeply than did the lesser ones. In presenting the evidence my purpose was—and, so far as may be, still remains—
to enable the reader to test any given case of Shakespearean
reminiscence by the whole body of the evidence. For this
reason, my essays set forth, *play by play*, all probable echoes
of that particular play in all of Milton's work. In presenting
the fresh illustrations of the present supplement,[3] I cannot
reprint the earlier materials, but, for those plays which are
echoed in the new materials, I have given in parentheses

1. *PMLA*, XL, 645-691.
2. Pp. 139-208 (cited hereafter as *SS*).
3. The texts used here are *The Complete Works of Shakespeare*, ed. G. L.
Kittredge (Boston, 1936), and *The Poems of John Milton*, ed. J. H. Hanford (New York, 1936). Just which of the early editions of Shakespeare
Milton may have used—or perhaps unconsciously collated?—can hardly be
determined; but textual variations in Shakespeare do not substantially affect
Milton's Shakespearean reminiscence.

after each title the total *number* of my earlier illustrations and a page reference thereto.[4] The new illustrations are numbered *in sequence* with those I have previously printed.

When last writing of these matters I foresaw, correctly, (1) that all of my illustrations might not necessarily commend themselves equally to every reader, and (2) that some other illustrations which might have been readily accepted had doubtless escaped me.[5] The main fact is, however, that my findings as a whole have won general acceptance. Meanwhile I have collected some of the items which had previously escaped me, and these are printed in the present supplement. They comprise nearly fifty fresh passages from Milton which illustrate once more, after due allowance is again made for possible coincidence or casual analogy,[6] his habitual closeness to Shakespeare. In presenting these additional illustrations I shall adhere to the arrangement I have previously described as follows:

Of many possible classifications only two seemed finally practicable. Some of the plays remained in Milton's memory not by virtue of their underlying dramatic concepts but

4. That is, to SS. The total numbers are given under two classifications, A and B, as explained below, pp. 81-82.
5. SS, p. 205, n. 2.
6. Some cases of *obviously* casual analogy are easily recognizable. For example, it is probably mere chance that Shakespeare and Milton give qualified approval, respectively, to "self-love" and to "self-esteem" *(Henry V* II.iv.74-75; *PL* VIII.571-572). Again, Shakespearean reminiscence is not needed to account for the fact that Milton matches Shakespeare's animadversions upon the multitude (the "giddy and unsure . . . vulgar heart," the "fond Many" of *2 Henry IV* I.iii.89-91) with the Saviour's sharp reflection, in *PR* III.49-51, upon "the people" as "a herd confused,/ A miscellaneous rabble who extol/ Things vulgar." Some cases, however, are not so clear. In the text, for example, I have not admitted a striking likeness between a famous line from *Hamlet* (I.iv.56) and an equally famous line from *PL* (II.148), though it can hardly be denied that Belial's "thoughts that wander through eternity" are, in one sense, strikingly analogous to Hamlet's "thoughts beyond the reaches of our souls." In this case it is not safe to assume that Milton necessarily remembered Shakespeare—but it is not easy to make up one's mind.

solely by the spell of the Shakespearean word or the fascination of their imagery. Such echoes or likenesses—of epithet, phrase, or figure: all essentially *verbal* or *figurative*, and very often both in one—I have brought together, play by play, in group A. Reminiscences or striking likenesses more essentially *dramatic* in nature—echoes of dramatic theme or mood, situation, or characterization—are presented play by play, in so far as they occur, in group B.[7]

These new materials give fresh support to the conclusions I have previously set forth,[8] because they demonstrate afresh the many subtle variations and the remarkable range of Shakespearean reminiscence in Milton.

Romeo and Juliet (A₅; pp. 144-146.)

A.

(6)II.ii.161-164:
Bondage is hoarse and may not speak aloud;
Else would I tear the cave where *Echo* lies,
And make her *airy tongue* more hoarse than mine
With repetition of my Romeo's *name*.

Comus 205-209 *(Just before the Lady sings her Echo song, she recalls):*
A thousand fantasies . . .
Of calling shapes and beckoning shadows dire,
And *airy tongues* that syllable men's *names*
On sands and shores and desert wildernesses.

---

7. *SS*, pp. 141-142 and *n.* The statement immediately following there is also pertinent here. I have independently collected the illustrations printed below, "but it goes without saying that I owe . . . much . . . aid and comfort to Milton's editors and commentators. All passages observed by them are noted *passim* . . . usually by initials appended to the passages from Milton." Thus, D = Dunster; W = Thomas Warton; T = Todd (variorum edition, 1809, which contains citations from these and many other commentators); Br. = R. C. Browne (*English Poems by John Milton*, Clarendon Press, 1923); M = Masson (*Poetical Works of John Milton*, London, 1903); V = A. W. Verity (ed. *Paradise Lost, Samson, Comus* [Cambridge, 1910], etc.).
8. *SS*, pp. 204-208.

(7)IV.i.45 *(Juliet to the Friar):*

Come weep with me—*past hope,* past cure, past help!

Samson Agonistes 120-121 *(The Chorus first sees Samson):*

As one *past hope,* abandoned,
And by himself given over.

(8)IV.i.81, 84; iii.40-45:
Or shut me nightly in a *charnel house* ...
Or bid me go into *a new-made grave.* ...
As in a *vault* ...
... where, as they say,
At some hours in the night *spirits resort.*

Comus 470-473:
Such are those thick and gloomy shadows damp
Oft seen in *charnel vaults* and sepulchres,
Lingering, and sitting by *a new-made grave*
As *loth to leave the body* that it loved.

B.

(1) Like Romeo and Juliet's good friar, the Genius of the Wood in *Arcades* makes his rounds at early dawn to visit and cherish his plants and flowers.

II.iii.1-18:
The grey-ey'd morn smiles on the frowning night ...
And flecked darkness like a drunkard reels
From forth day's path. ...
Now, ere the sun advance his burning eye ...
I must up-fill this osier cage of ours
With baleful weeds and precious-juiced flowers.
... from [earth's] womb children of divers kind
We sucking on her natural bosom find;

Arcades 48-60:
... all my plants I save from nightly ill ...
And from the boughs brush off the evil dew,
And heal the harms of thwarting thunder blue,
Or what the cross dire-looking planet smites. ...
And early ere the odorous breath of morn
Awakes the slumbering leaves, or tasselled horn

Many for many virtues
    excellent. . . .
For naught so vile that on
    the earth doth live
But to the earth some special
    good doth give.

Shakes the high thicket,
    haste I all about,
Number my ranks, and visit
    every sprout
With puissant words and
    murmurs made to
    bless.

Hamlet (A₁₃ B₅; pp. 148-155.)
A.

(14) III.i.51-53:
The *harlot's cheek*, beautied
    with plast'ring art,
Is not more ugly to the thing
    that helps it
Than is my deed to my most
    painted word.

Paradise Regained IV.343-
344:
. . . their *swelling epithets*
    thick laid
As *varnish* on a *harlot's
    cheek*.—(D)

(15) I.ii.133-134:
How *weary*, stale, *flat*, and
    unprofitable
Seem to me all the uses of
    this world!

SA 594-596:
So much I feel *my genial
    spirits droop*,
My hopes all *flat;* Nature
    within me *seems*
In all her functions *weary*
    of herself.—(M)[9]

(16) V.ii.358:
Absent thee from *felicity*
    awhile,
And in this harsh world
    draw thy breath *in
    pain*,
To tell my story.

*Epitaph on the Marchioness
of Winchester*, 61-68:
Whilst thou, bright Saint,
    high sitt'st in glory,
Next her, much like to thee
    in story,
[Joseph's mother, who] at
    her next birth, much
    like thee
Through pangs fled to
    felicity.[10]

9. Cf. SS, pp. 153, 166.
10. This *Epitaph* also echoes unmistakably a song from *Cymbeline* (cf.
SS, p. 196).

(17) My previous study[11] presented evidence to show that Milton remembered the "thoughts, deeds, and words" of certain outstanding characters of this play, including the words of the Ghost in his opening colloquy with Hamlet. If my ear does not deceive me, the *cadence*[12] of another great line in the Ghost's speech seems to have echoed and re-echoed in Milton's memory, and thereafter, with Miltonic variations, in the memory of other English poets.

I.v.76-77 *(The elder Hamlet was):*
Cut off even in the blossoms
    of my sin,
Unhous'led, disappointed, unanel'd.

Paradise Lost II.185; V.899:
*Unrespited, unpitied,
    unreprieved....
Unshaken, unseduced,
    unterrified.*

PR III.429:
*Unhumbled, unrepentant,
    unreformed.*

Note also: Pope's "unwept, unhonour'd, uninterr'd";[13] Scott's "unwept, unhonour'd, and unsung";[14] Byron's "unknell'd, uncoffin'd, and unknown";[15] and Browning's "ignoble, insufficient, incomplete."[16] One word more as regards the cadence. In Shaw's *Dark Lady of the Sonnets* the Beefeater asks, "What manner of thing is a cadence, sir?" To which the

11. *SS*, p. 150.
12. I think it was Shakespeare's *cadence* that took the ear of the later poets. This in spite of the fact, noted by Thyer and Todd (see Todd, II, 387), that some of the Greek tragedians and some English poets before Shakespeare had—with sundry *differing* cadences—used "this way of introducing several adjectives beginning with the same letter, without any conjunction"—as in Spenser's "unbodied, unsoul'd, unheard, unseen" *(FQ* VII. vii.46) and Fairfax's "unseen, unmark'd, unpitied, unrewarded" *(Tasso* II. xvi). Later editors who comment on the *Hamlet* passage in connection with *PL* II.185 include Browne, Verity, and F. A. Patterson *(The Student's Milton*, New York, 1933).
13. *Iliad* XXII.484.
14. *Lay of the Last Minstrel* VI.i.
15. *Childe Harold* IV.179.
16. *Luria* IV.190.

Man (Shakespeare) replies, once for all, "A thing to rule the world with, friend."[17]

B.

(6) The passionate attachment—strengthened by mutual guilt—between King Claudius and Gertrude, is analogous to that between Adam and Eve after the fall. The two men state the case in similar terms.

IV.vii.14:
She's so *conjunctive* to my
    life and *soul*
That, as the star moves not
    but in his sphere,
I could not but by her.

PL IX 952-958:
... I with thee have fixed
    my lot ... if death
Consort with thee, *death*
    is to me as life ...
Our state cannot be severed;
    we are one.

Othello (A₄ B₂; pp. 155-158.)

A.

(5)V.ii.277-281:
Whip me, ye devils. . . .
Blow me about in *winds!*
    roast me in sulphur!
Wash me in steep-down
    gulfs of liquid *fire!*
O Desdemona, Desdemona!
    dead!

PL III.487-488; II.598-603:
A violent cross *wind* ...
Blows them transverse ten
    thousand leagues
    awry.
... the bitter change/Of
    fierce extremes ...
From beds of raging *fire* to
    starve in *ice*
... thence hurried back to
    fire.[18]

17. G. B. Shaw, *Misalliance, The Dark Lady, Fanny's First Play,* (London, 1914), p. 135.
18. Milton's lines are also close to *Measure for Measure* III.i.83-85, 118-128 (cf. *SS,* pp. 194-195).

B.

(3) A twice-repeated phrase of Othello's to Desdemona, in response to her plea for Cassio just before Iago undermines Othello's faith in her—and possibly another famous phrase from Othello's last speech, again concerning his love for Desdemona—seem to be echoed in Samson's reproach to Dalila.

III.iii.70-83; V.ii.344:

Desd. What, Michael Cassio,
That came a-wooing
          with you . . .
. . . to have so much to do
To bring him in?. . .
Oth. . . .Let him come
         when he will!
I will deny thee nothing!
Desd. Why, this is not
         a boon.
'Tis as I should entreat you
        wear your gloves. . . .
Oth. I will *deny thee*
        nothing!

. . . one that *lov'd* not wisely,
    but *too well.*

SA 876-881:

I before all the daughters of
    my tribe
And of my nation chose thee
    from among
My enemies, *loved* thee, as
    too well thou knew'st,
Too well, unbosomed all my
    secrets to thee,
Not out of levity, but over-
    powered
By thy request, who could
    deny thee nothing.

Macbeth (A₇ B₃; pp. 161-166.)

A.

(8) I.vi.1-6:

        The *air*
Nimbly and sweetly recom-
    mends itself
Unto our gentle senses./
    . . . the heaven's
    breath

Nativity Ode 32-33, 37-38:

Nature . . ./ Had doffed her
    gaudy trim. . . .
Only with speeches fair
She *woos* the *gentle air.*[19]

19. A similar passage in *Romeo and Juliet* I.iv.100 is noted in *SS*, p. 145.

Smells *wooingly* here.

Comus 3-9:
... bright aerial spirits live
insphered ...
Above the smoke and stir[20]
of this dim spot
Which men call Earth, and
with low-thoughted
care,
Confined and pestered in
this pinfold here,

(9) III.ii.22-23:
Duncan is in his grave;
After *life's fitful fever* he
sleeps well.

Strive to keep up a *frail and
feverish being,*
Unmindful of the crown that
Virtue gives.

Wordsworth and Keats, in turn, remembered Shakespeare
and Milton ("life's fitful fever" and "the smoke and stir of
this dim ... Earth") in "Tintern Abbey" ("the fretful stir/
Unprofitable, and the fever of the world") and in the "Ode
to a Nightingale" ("The weariness, the fever, and the fret/
Here, where men sit and hear each other groan").

B.

(4) V.viii.46-50 *(Siward in-
quires concerning his son's
death in battle):*
Had he his hurts before?
Ross.   Ay, on the front.
Siward.   Why then, God's
soldier be he!
Had I as many sons as I have
hairs,
I would not wish them to a
fairer death.
And so his knell is knoll'd.

SA 1579-1589, 1708-1717
*(Manoa asks the Messenger
about Samson's death):*
How died he? death to life
is crown or shame. . . .
Messenger. Unwounded of
his enemies he fell.
.../ The edifice . . .
Upon their heads and on his
own he pulled. . . .
Manoa. Come, come, no time
for lamentation now,

20. Verity *(Comus,* 1921, p. 46) thinks that Milton's "smoke and stir" is
"an echo perhaps of Horace's famous ... '*fumum et opes strepitumque
Romae.*'"

> Nor much more cause. Sam-
> son hath quit himself
> Like Samson, and heroicly
> hath finished
> A life heroic. . . .
> To himself and father's
> house eternal fame.

Timon of Athens (A₃; p. 166.)

B.

(1) Timon and Samson are both bitterly disillusioned in their friendships.

(At first Timon thinks him-self "wealthy in my friends [II.ii.193], *only to recognize, before long):*
"the monstrousness of man When he looks out in an un-grateful shape" (III.ii. 79-80).

(He rails bitterly at these fair-weather friends): "such summer birds are men," "mouth-friends," "trencher friends" (III.vi.34, 99, 106).

SA 187-193:
         . . . I learn
Now of my own experience, not by talk
How counterfeit a coin they are who "friends"
Bear in their superscription (of the most
I would be understood). In prosperous days
They swarm, but in adverse withdraw their head
Not to be found, though sought.

Antony and Cleopatra (A₅ B₃; pp. 166-168.)

A.

(6) I.v.24-27:
         He's speaking now,
Or murmuring 'Where's my serpent of old Nile?'
For so he calls me. Now I

Comus 524-527 *(The en-chanter):*
. . . to every thirsty wanderer
By sly enticement gives his baneful cup,

feed myself
With most *delicious poison.*

With many murmurs mixed,
whose *pleasing poison*
The visage quite transforms
of him that drinks.[21]

(7) My earlier citation of evidence[22] showed that the character of Cleopatra made "deep impression" upon Milton. One aspect of her fascination is unforgettably described in the great speech of Enorbarbus concerning her inexhaustible but unsatiating allure. This, by a curious transference, seems to reappear in the remarks of Adam to Raphael, concerning his insatiable desire to hear more of the Angel's gracious discourse of God and man.

II.ii.240-243:
Age cannot wither her nor
    custom stale
Her infinite variety. Other
    women *cloy*
The appetites they feed, but
    she makes hungry
Where most she satisfies.

PL VIII.211-216:
. . . sweeter thy discourse is
    to my ear
Than fruits of palm-tree,
    pleasantest to thirst
And hunger both . . . *they*
    satiate and soon fill,
Though pleasant, but thy
    words, with grace
    divine
Imbued, *bring to their*
    sweetness no satiety.

Richard III (A₁₀ B₂; pp. 170-173.)

A.

(11)V.iii.312:
Our strong arms be our con-
    science, *swords our*
    law!

PL XI.671-672; IX.653-654:
        . . . so violence
Proceeded, and oppression,
    and *sword-law.*—(T)[23]
        . . . we live
Law to ourselves; our reason
    is *our law.*

21. Cf. below, p. 92, under *King John.*
22. SS, pp. 167-168.
23. Cf. SS, p. 171.

(12) II.ii.151-152:
My *other self,* my counsel's
    consistory,
My oracle, my prophet.

PL VIII.450:
  ... thy *other self,*[24]
Thy wish exactly to thy
    heart's desire.

B.

(3) The brazen wit with which Richard so jauntily assails his prospective victims also inspires the efforts of Comus and Satan (in *PR*) to bedazzle their intended victims.

IV.i.79-80; I.ii.49-50, 81-84, 114-115 *(Though ultimately, as Anne reports, her):*
    woman's heart
Grossly grew captive to his
    honey words,
(originally, seeing through him, she had repelled his advances with a sharp riposte for his every thrust):
Richard. Sweet saint, for
    charity, be not so
    curst.
Anne. Foul devil, for God's
    sake hence, and
    trouble us not! ...
Richard. Fairer than tongue
    can name thee, let me
    have
Some patient leisure to
    excuse myself.
Anne. Fouler than heart can
    think thee, thou canst
    make
No excuse current but to
    hang thyself. ...

Comus 789-791 *(The Lady refuting Comus):*
Enjoy your *dear wit and gay rhetoric*
That hath so well been
    taught her dazzling
    fence;
Thou art not fit to hear
    thyself convinced.

PR IV.2-5:
The Tempter stood ...
Discovered in his fraud,
    thrown from his
    hope
So oft, and the persuasive
    rhetoric
That sleeked his tongue.

24. The "classical" *alter ego?*

Richard.   But, gentle Lady
     Anne,
To leave *this keen encounter*
     of our wits. . . .

King John (A₂ B₁; pp. 173-174.)

A.

| (3)I.i.213:
Sweet, sweet, *sweet poison*
     for the age's tooth. | *Comus* 47:
. . . the *sweet poison* of
     misusëd wine.[25] |

Richard II (A₇ B₂; pp. 174-175.)

A.

(8)II.iv.9-15:
. . . *meteors* fright the fixed
     stars of heaven;
The pale-fac'd moon looks
     bloody on the earth,
And lean-look'd prophets
     whisper *fearful*
     change. . . .
These signs forerun the
     death or *fall of kings.*

PL I.594-599:
. . . the sun new-risen
Looks through the hori-
     zontal misty air
Shorn of his beams, or from
     behind the moon
In *dim eclipse* disastrous
     twilight sheds
On half the nations, and
     with *fear of change*
Perplexes monarchs.

(9)II.iv.18-20:
Ah, Richard! . . .
I see thy glory, *like a shoot-*
     ing star,
Fall to the base earth from
     the firmament.[26]

PL IV.555-556; I.740-746:
Thither came Uriel, gliding
     through the even
On a sun beam, *swift as a*
     shooting star.[27]
(*Mulciber*, "*thrown by an-*

25. Cf. above, p. 90, under *Antony and Cleopatra.*
26. See also below, p. 96, item 17, and SS, p. 187.
27. Todd (II, 364) suggests that Milton might have "adapted" this simile directly from Theocritus (*Idyll* XIII.49), but it seems likely that he remembered it more immediately as a favorite of Shakespeare's.

gry Jove" over "the crystal
battlements" of heaven):
Dropped from the zenith
    like a falling star,
On Lemnos the Aegæan
    isle.

I Henry IV (A₅ B₃; pp. 176-178.)

B.

(4) In my previous studies[28] I have noted an echo, in *PL*
II.533-534, of King Henry's memorable opening speech. I
now find that two additional phrases, both from that part
of the same great speech in which the king pays tribute to
the Master, were in young Milton's mind in 1629—a year
before his lines "On Shakespeare"—when he wrote his
Nativity Ode.

I.i.18-27:

        Therefore, friends,
As far as to the sepulchre of
        Christ—
Whose soldier now, under
        whose blessed cross
We are impressed and en-
        gag'd to fight . . .
To chase these pagans in
        those holy fields
Over whose acres walk'd
        those *blessed feet*
Which fourteen hundred
        years ago were nail'd

Nativity Ode 23-25, 151-153:
The star-led Wizards haste
        with odors sweet!

O run, prevent them with
        thy humble ode,
And lay it lowly at his
        blessed feet. . . .

The Babe lies yet in smiling
        infancy
That on the *bitter cross*[29]
Must redeem our loss.

---

28. *SS*, p. 176.

29. Neither "blessed feet" nor "bitter cross" is biblical.—I find that R. C.
Browne noticed "the bitter cross" (I, 258: "Cf. Shakespeare, 'For our
advantage to the bitter cross'"), but not the significant compound echo in
"his blessed feet."

For our advantage on the
     bitter cross.

2 Henry IV (A₃ B₂; pp. 178-180.)

A.

(4) The first passages from Shakespeare and Milton in the following group are reprinted here[30] because they become more clearly recognizable notes of a compound echo when read together with the remaining two passages, not hitherto noted, both of which hark back to the same great speech at the opening of *2 Henry IV* III.

III.i.5-8, 9-13:
     O sleep, O *gentle sleep!*
Nature's *soft* nurse, how have
     I frighted thee,
That thou no more wilt weigh
     my eyelids down
And *steep my senses in for-
     getfulness?*

Why rather, sleep, liest thou
     in *smoky cribs,*
Upon uneasy pallets stretch-
     ing thee . . .
*Than in the perfum'd cham-
     bers of* the great,
Under the canopies of costly
     state. . . .

PL VIII.287-289:
     . . . there *gentle sleep*
First found me, and with
     soft oppression
     seized
My *drowsed sense.*

Comus 321-325:
     . . . I . . ./trust thy honest-
     offered courtesy,
Which oft is sooner found
     in *lowly sheds*
With *smoky rafters, than in
     tapestry halls*
And courts of princes.

30. From *SS*, p. 179.

Two Gentlemen of Verona (A₂; p. 183.)

A.

(3)III.i.219-220:
O, I have fed *upon this woe*
    already,
And now excess of it will
    make me *surfeit.*

SA 1558-1562 *(The Messen-
ger to Manoa):*
Gaza yet stands, but all her
    sons are fallen. . . .
Feed on that first, there may
    in *grief* be *surfeit.—*
    (Br.)

A Midsummer Night's Dream (A₁₃ B₃; pp. 183-188.)

A.

(14)II.i.99-100 *(Because of
the fairies' dissension):*
. . . the *quaint* mazes in the
    wanton green
For lack of tread are undis-
    tinguishable.

Arcades 44-47:
    . . . I am the Power
Of this fair wood . . . and
    curl the grove
With *ringlets quaint* and
    wanton windings
    wove.—(W)

(15)III.i.163-164 *(Titania to*
Bottom):
And I will *purge* thy *mortal
    grossness* so
That thou shalt like an airy
    spirit go.

Arcades 72-73:
. . . the heavenly tune, which
    none can hear
Of *human mould* with *gross
    unpurged ear.—*(W)

(16)I.i.184-185:
More tuneable than lark to
    shepherd's ear.

PR I.479-480:
    . . . pleasing to the ear
And *tuneable* as sylvan pipe
    or song.—(D)

PL V.151:
More tuneable than . . . lute
    or harp.

(17)II.i.153, 7:
And certain *stars shot* madly
      from their spheres.

Swifter than the moonës
      sphere.

Comus 80-81:
Swift as the sparkle of a
      glancing star
I *shoot* from heaven.[31]

B.

(4) Shakespeare's memorable concept of the shaping power of the creative imagination is recalled in the thought and phrasing of a passage in *PL*.

V.i.14-17:
   ... as *imagination* bodies
      forth
The forms of *things* unknown,
      the poet's pen
Turns them to *shapes,* and
      gives to *airy* nothing
A local habitation and a
      name.

PL V.100-105 *(Adam lectures Eve on the nature of the soul's faculties, of which Reason is "chief," and):*
                     Fancy next
Her office holds; of all external *things* ...
She forms *imaginations, airy shapes.*[32]

Merchant of Venice (A₄; pp. 188-189.)

A.

(5)V.i.56-57, 60-65, 79:
   Soft *stillness and the night*
Become the touches of sweet
      harmony....

There's not the *smallest orb*
      which thou behold'st

Arcades 61-64, 68-73:
   ... *in deep of night* ... then
      listen I
To the *celestial sirens'*
      harmony,
That sit upon the nine enfolded *spheres....*

---

31. Cf. above, p. 92, item 9.—Todd (VI, 253) compares *Venus and Adonis* 815: "Look how a bright star shooteth from the sky."
32. Cf. above, p. 82, item 6.

But in his motion like an
    angel sings . . .
Such harmony is in immortal
    souls;
But *whilst this muddy ves-
    ture of decay*
Doth *grossly close it in, we
    cannot* hear it. . . .

. . . the *sweet power* of *music.*

Such *sweet compulsion* doth
    in *music* lie
To . . . keep unsteady Nature
    to her law,
And the low world in meas-
    ured motion draw
After *the heavenly tune,*
    which *none can hear*
Of human mould with *gross
    unpurged* ear.[33]

Comus 457-458:
And in clear dream and
    solemn vision
Tell her of things that no
    gross ear can hear.

As You Like It (A₅; pp. 190-191.)

A.

(6) III.ii.420-425, 446:
Rosalind. Love is merely a
    madness. . . . Yet I
    profess curing it. . . .
Orlando. I *would not be
    cured.* . . .

Elegy VII 87-88, 99:
O utinam spectare semel
    mihi detur amatos
Vultus, et coràm tristia
    verba loqui. . . .
Deme meos tandem, verùm
    nec deme, furores.
(Oh, that I may have the
privilege of seeing once
again that beloved face and
of telling her my sad tale.
. . . Take away *my madness,*
I pray; or rather, *do not take
it away.*—N. G. McCrea's
translation.)[34]

---

33. Cf*l* above, p. 95, item 15.—Thomas Warton had noted the likeness
between the second of the three passages quoted from Shakespeare and
the last two lines of the passage from *Arcades.* (Cf. *SS,* p. 188, n. 2.)

34. Quoted from Patterson, pp. 93-94.

Twelfth Night (A₂; p. 191.)

A.

(3) I.v.82:
Infirmity, that *decays the
        wise* ...

Lycidas 70-71:
Fame is the spur that the
        clear spirit doth
        raise
(That last *infirmity* of *noble
        mind*) ... [35]

Pericles (A₁; p. 195.)

A.

(2) Gower, Prologue, 21-24:
This king unto him took a
        feere,
Who died and left a female
        heir,
So buxom, blithe, and full of
        face
As heaven had lent her all
        his grace.

L'Allegro 19-24:
Zephyr with Aurora playing,
As he met her once
        a-Maying ...
Filled her with thee, a
        daughter fair,
So buxom, blithe, and
        debonair.—(W)

Cymbeline (A₂ B₃; pp. 196-198.)

B.

(4) I have previously[36] called attention to the fact that
Satan in *Paradise Lost* "belongs to a tradition which includes Iachimo as well as Iago." A passage from *Comus*
should be added to the supporting evidence. Like Iachimo
when he sees the sleeping Imogen, Satan (*PL* IX.457-469),

35. R. C. Browne (I, 301) compares Tacitus (*Hist.* IV.5): "Etiam
sapientibus cupido gloriae novissima exuitur."
36. In *SS*, pp. 197-198.

literally hell-bent upon bringing ruin to the unsuspecting Eve, is genuinely moved, and, for a moment, deterred from his wickedness while gazing upon her helpless grace and innocence. So, too, is Comus, on seeing and hearing the Lady sing her Echo song.

II.ii.14-23, 49-50:

Cytherea,
How bravely thou becom'st
 thy bed! fresh lily,
And whiter than the sheets!
 That I might touch!
But kiss; one kiss. . . .
To see th' enclosed lights,
 now canopied
Under these windows white
 and azure, lac'd
With blue of heaven's own
 tinct!
 . . . I lodge in fear.
Though this a heavenly
 angel, hell is here.

Comus 246-248, 262-264:

Sure something holy lodges
 in that breast,
And with these raptures
 moves the vocal air
To testify his hidden resi-
 dence. . . .
. . . such a sacred and home-
 felt delight,
Such sober certainty of
 waking bliss,
I never heard till now. I'll
 speak to her,
And she shall be my queen.[37]

The Tempest (A₆ B₅; pp. 198-202.)

A.

(7) I.ii.321-323:
As *wicked dew* as e'er my
 mother *brush'd*
With raven's feather from
 unwholesome fen
Drop on you both!

Arcades 48-51:
. . . all my plants I save from
 nightly ill . . .
And from the boughs *brush*
 off the *evil* dew,[38]
And heal the harms of
 thwarting thunder
 blue.

37. Cf. also SS, pp. 200-201.
38. "The expression and idea are Shakespearean, but in a different sense and application" (Warton, in Todd, VI, 163). See also above, p. 83, item 1.

THOMAS B. STROUP

Lycidas *and the* Marinell Story

IT IS OFTEN INTERESTING and sometimes enlightening to apply an artist's theory of the creation, or the basic assumption of his theory, to that same artist's works. Such application, at least as a starting point toward the understanding of what he wrote, is justified, and its implications would seem to be worth some consideration. Now, Milton adhered to a widely known, if not generally accepted, theory of the creation, one that is as applicable to the creative process employed by man as to that employed by God: creation does not take place *ex nihilo*. Rather, it consists in bringing order out of chaos, in bringing shape to what is shapeless, in imposing upon material the form the creator desires. Thus, the poet as creator, to follow Milton's logic, builds, not from airy nothing, but from nature, from the many materials stored in his mind by experience, the experience of reading among the rest. They constitute what Professor Woodhouse aptly calls the poet's "intellectual frame of reference."

These materials, if one may follow the theory further, are sometimes consciously employed, as when the poet deliberately reshapes a story he has read or heard; sometimes they are rather accidentally or semiconsciously used, as when the poet introduces a situation, an image, or a phrase which reveals by implication merely his reading or a special body of his experience.[1] Most frequently the two are com-

1. For instance, it is very possible Milton was not aware at the moment he wrote that he was paraphrasing Job xxxviii.4-11 in the *Nativity Ode*:

bined, for it is not often that the poet (the artist) deliberately
and consciously borrows his story, for instance, and as consciously borrows also each part by which he re-shapes it
into a new work. To separate the deliberate and conscious
from the accidental and semi- or un- conscious in the study
of a poet's work is difficult under any circumstances and
perhaps not very profitable. Yet to find in the work of the
poet evidences especially of what may be the accidental
or the semiconscious employment of identifiable materials
gives, by allusion at least, a richness to the work it has not
enjoyed hitherto, sometimes clarifies its meaning, and not
infrequently reveals something of the character of the creator. And even though the materials may not be absolutely
identifiable, even though the parallels or allusions seem tenuous as such, the student is in duty called upon to point them
out: other minds, making additional associations, may bring
to a surety what was little more than a conjecture; or they
may, thus stimulated, come upon different and yet more
valid conclusions.

A group of such allusive materials appears, I believe, in
Lycidas, perhaps without the poet's conscious realization of
their having already been loosely assembled elsewhere. They
seem to be embedded, as it were, deep within the poem,
showing themselves only as occasional outcroppings of
names, situations, images, phrases, and cadences. Yet they are
hardly in the poem by mere accident, for there are too many
of them, and Milton was too familiar with the work in which

"But when of old the Sons of Morning Sung." His attention called to it,
however, he would have immediately acknowledged his indebtedness.

Milton's theory serves here as a justification and a starting point merely.
Its implications are obvious. I am not concerned with his complex theory
of art and poetic. The materials are presented as a sample of the poet's
ordering his art-stuff. See *De doctrina* I.vii; and such works as A. S. P.
Woodhouse, "Milton's Views on the Creation," *PQ*, XXVIII (1949), 211 ff.
(especially sect. 2); Maurice Kelley, *This Great Argument* (Princeton, 1941),
pp. 122 ff.; and Douglas Bush, *English Literature in the Earlier Seventeenth
Century, 1600-1660* (Oxford, 1945), pp. 382, 388.

they may be found. They constitute, I believe, still another body of rich material lying back of that infinitely rich poem.

A reading of *Lycidas* will readily impress one, perhaps not so much with the high lawns or the oaks or the stretched out hills, as with the remarkable amount of sea imagery and the poet's great dependence upon personages and places associated with the sea for much of the richness of allusion and meaning. The sea nymphs, Orpheus, Arethusa and Mincius, Alpheus, Triton, Aeolus and the daughters of Nereus, Camus, the dolphins, even "the Pilot of the *Galilean* lake"—all are associated with the waters; and the body of the drowned upon its watery bier visits the "bottom of the monstrous world," or lies beyond the Hebrides, or is washed far away. Indeed, the drowned shepherd, gaining immortality, becomes himself the genius of the shore—an Alpheus, a Camus, a Palaemon, or a St. Peter. These references, calling the reader's mind to the rich myths of the rivers and the seas, are beautifully fitting to the subject and to the occasion, and one of the triumphs of the poem. This body of sea materials, no doubt, rose to the surface of the poet's mind from many places, came to him out of many experiences.

What seems to have been one of these places, and one that has apparently not been suggested, is a part of the Marinell-Florimell story of the *Faerie Queene*.[2] One finds

2. Milton's frequent allusions to Spenser are a commonplace of English scholarship. Reference to the Marinell story is to be found even in his *History of Britain*. (See *The Spenser Variorum, Faerie Queene*, Book III, p. 238.) J. H. Hanford, "The Pastoral Elegy and Milton's *Lycidas*," *PMLA*, XXV (1910), 403-417, shows specifically Milton's very substantial indebtedness to the *Shepheardes Calender*, especially to the May, July, and September Eclogues. The October has a short passage on fame that reminds one of the passage on fame in *Lycidas*. Hanford considers Spenser a direct source for *Lycidas*. L. S. Friedland shows rather convincingly ("*Lycidas* and Spenser's *Ruines of Time*," *MLN*, XXVII [1912], 246-250) that Milton echoes the *Ruines of Time* in *Lycidas*. What appear to be reflections of Spenser's words, images, and ideas in Milton's works may all be valid,

most of the suggestive materials in III.iv, but a few as Spenser returns to the story in III.viii and IV.xi-xii. Most suggestive of *Lycidas* is that part following Britomart's complaint about the shipwreck of her "feeble bark" and her overthrow of Marinell, guardian of the shore. It deals with the coming of Marinell's mother Cymoent and her sisters to lament for him and take him away in their dolphin-drawn chariot to the bottom of the seas, where they minister to him. There seem to be also a few allusions in the succeeding account of Marinell's recovery of his health through Apollo's intervention, of his releasing the true Florimell from Proteus' person, and of his winning her hand. Immediately, rather obvious comparisons come to mind, not all of them suggested by the Orpheus myth,[3] the Nereides, and the other classical sea materials in the two poems. There are more, and the similarities will become more apparent if given in some detail. Perhaps they can be most readily realized if presented, not according to a classification into types, but as they come in their narrative sequence in the *Faerie Queene*. They are not so much verbal similarities, though these occur, as similar situations, similar phrasing and tone, and similar images.

An early suggestion in *Lycidas* lies in the pastoral formula "Where were ye nymphs?" which calls to mind the sea and the particular scene in the *Faerie Queene* (III.iv.29-30) in which Cymoent and her attendants hear of Marinell's mishap:

---

though they repeat each other, or though the reflection comes ultimately from a classical or some other precedent source. Milton's mind fused several bodies of material and brought forth the unique product.

3. Recent scholarship has made much of the Orpheus myth in *Lycidas* (see Caroline W. Mayerson, "The Orpheus Image in *Lycidas*," *PMLA*, LXIV [1949], 189-207). Quotations from *Lycidas* herein follow the 1645 edition, as reprinted in *The Poetical Works of John Milton*, ed. H. C. *Beeching* (New York, 1938).

Which when his mother deare did vnderstond,
And heauy tydings heard, whereas she playd
Amongst her watry sisters by a pond,
Gathering sweet daffadillyes, to haue made
Gay girlonds, from the sun their forheads faire to shade;

xxx

Eftsoones both flowres and girlonds farre away
She flong, and her faire deawy lockes yrent,
To sorrow huge she turnd her former play,
And gamesom merth to grieuous dreriment:[4]

The passage also suggests the later lines in *Lycidas* in which Aeolus (Hippotades) explains that the air was calm and that *"Panope* with all her sisters [they who should have been looking after the shepherd] play'd" on the level brine at the time of Lycidas' drowning. It calls to one's mind the brilliant flower passage. But more especially the pictures, the imagery called up, in the *Faerie Queene* are like those in *Lycidas:* Cymoent plays among her sisters as Panope does among hers; the nymphs should have been playing near by when the deep closed over Marinell's head, just as Panope and her sisters should have been near.

As soon as Cymoent hears of Marinell's misadventure, she, grief-stricken and quite beside herself, makes her way by dolphin chariot ("A teme of dolphins, raunged in aray") to the shore where her loved Marinell lies; and when she takes him, seemingly dead, to her home in the sea caves, it is in this same dolphin-drawn vehicle. Ultimately he, having recovered life at the intervention of the gods, like Palaemon, is restored to his rule of the shore. Lycidas' body, if the

4. An earlier image suggestive of *Lycidas* is the bark in Britomart's complaint before she subdues Marinell. Her "Feeble barke" is the basic metaphor of the lament, and the fear of shipwreck and drowning the metaphorical theme. (See III.iv.8-10.) All quotations from the *Faerie Queene* are taken from the J. C. Smith edition (Oxford, 1909).

shepherd-poet is heeded, is carried by a similar team: "And, O Ye *Dolphins,* waft the haples youth." And he, likewise restored, becomes ultimately the genius of the shore.

Now, most of the annotators of *Lycidas* cite as the source of this line the well-known myth of Arion. According to Herodotus, when Arion was cast overboard by sailors a dolphin, having been called up by his music (dolphins are notably fond of man and man's music, according to Pliny), gladly carried the young musician safe to shore.[5] Arion's story is in some measure appropriate in that he, like Lycidas, was a musician-poet. Much more appropriate, however, is the Palaemon myth, as T. O. Mabbott has recently shown.[6] He reminds us that, contrary to later editors, Richardson and Newton noted that the dolphin reference in *Lycidas* is to the Palaemon myth. He points out further that this reference fits far better than the Arion myth: Palaemon was a youth who was drowned with his crazed mother as she was trying to save him and herself from his maddened father; his body was brought to shore near Corinth by a friendly dolphin and there buried by Sysiphus (according to Pausanias), and there a temple and statue were raised in his honor. Thus he became the guardian of the shore. According to Ovid's version of the myth, Venus took pity on Ino and her son, and persuaded Neptune to turn the two of them into gods—Palaemon and Leucothoë. Thus the Palaemon myth fits more closely both the Spenser story and the Milton reference than does the Arion. And if Milton remembered either of these myths (and probably both flitted

5. Herodotus, tr. A. D. Godley, (4 vols. London, 1921), I, 25-29, sects. 23-24. See also the *Attic Nights* of Aulus Gellius, XVI.xix. In Geffrey Whitney's *A Choice of Emblemes, and Other Devises* (Leyden, 1586), one finds (in "The Second Part," p. 142) a poem that tells the story and a woodcut illustrative of it.

6. T. O. Mabbott, "Milton's *Lycidas,* Lines 164 and 183-185," *Explicator,* V (1947), item 26. See Pausanias II.i, ii, and Ovid's *Metamorphoses* IV.531 ff., for references to the story. Milton refers directly to the Palaemon story in *Comus,* 875, and Spenser, in *FQ* IV.xi.13.

through his mind as he wrote), he also remembered, willy-nilly, Spenser's display of "new fiction of his own coinage" (to quote from Warton's comments on Spenser's method of handling myth) in the Marinell story. (Indeed Spenser's story of Marinell was very probably stimulated by the same myth.) The guardian nymphs common to both Milton and Spenser do not appear in either of the myths; indeed, in neither of the myths is there more than one dolphin for the youth to ride, but in Spenser and in Milton there are two or more. These singular similarities clinch the connection.

The possibility, if not the probability, of the connection is enhanced by what takes place when Cymoent finds her son. Before she and her sisters carry away the body of Marinell, she utters her complaint on fame and on the seeming fruitlessness of immortal life:

> *Deare image of my selfe (she sayd) that is,*
> *The wretched sonne of wretched mother borne,*
> *Is this thine high aduancement, O is this*
> *Th' immortall name, with which thee yet vnborne*
> *Thy Gransire* Nereus *promist to adorne?*
>
> (III.iv.36)

> . . . .
>
> *O what auailes it of immortall seed*
> *To beene ybred and neuer borne to die?*
> *Farre better I it deeme to die with speed,*
> *Then waste in woe and wailefull miserie.*
> *Who dyes the vtmost dolour doth abye,*
> *But who that liues, is left to waile his losse:*
> *So life is losse, and death felicitie. . . .*
>
> (III.iv.38)

> . . . .
>
> *But if the heauens did his dayes enuie,*
> *And my short blisse maligne, yet mote they well. . . .*
>
> (III.iv.39)

Not only is the theme here close to the theme of fame in
Lycidas, but the words in *Lycidas* seem to echo those in the
Faerie Queene:

> *Alas! What boots it with uncessant care*
> *To tend the homely slighted Shepherds trade,...*
> *Were it not better don as others use,...*

Or later:

> Fame *is no plant that grows on mortal soil,*
> *Nor in the glistering foil...*
> *But lives and spreds aloft by those pure eyes....*
> (*Lycidas* 64-65, 66, 78-79 81)

Here is a difference, to be sure. No doubt the theme of fame
touched Milton closely as a young poet. Yet the fact that
the subject did touch him personally is good warrant that
he would remember the many wise words he had read on
the subject and that he would recall these words when he
came to express himself on it. Assuredly this almost defiant
lament from Spenser is in tone like the outburst in *Lycidas.*
The "what-boots-it?" rhetorical question followed immediately by the "far better" rhetorical reply in both argues a
connection.

Other situations and phrasings are alike also. Marinell,
half god, has a sort of immortality, but a sort that is un-
satisfactory without the immortality of name and deed;
Lycidas, capable of creating a name by worthy deeds, is
to all human appearances cut off from name and fame by
death. In both cases, however, true immortality is to be
gained through other means than human: the eternal powers
must intervene. In both cases, moreover, it appears to the
mourners, if only momentarily, that the heavens have envied
them their dear ones and that the powers above are to blame
for the loss. We know, of course, that the discrediting of

fame was not uncommon in the literature of the time; yet the similarity here, the especial connection in both cases with immortality, makes it seem very likely that Milton's mind in ordering his material went back, consciously or not, to his intellectual frame of reference, which most certainly included the effective treatment of the theme in these lines of Spenser. Here Milton's short outburst seems to reflect Spenser's much more extensive treatment of the subject in the lament.

Following her lament, Cymoent and her maids take up the body of Marinell to place it in the chariot. In so doing

> *They softly wipt away the gelly blood*
> *From th' orifice; which hauing well vpbound,*
> *They pourd in soueraine balme, and Nectar good,*
> *Good both for earthly med'cine, and for heauenly food.*
>
> (III.iv.40)

Thus the nymphs minister to the youth. The passage suggests a brilliant transformation on Milton's part: "And wipe the tears for ever from his eyes." But the peculiarity that seems to make certain a connection between the poems here lies in the use of nectar as a medicine, for Lycidas "With *Nectar* pure his oozy Locks he laves." Moreover, Liagore, a nymph who "had learned skill/ In leaches craft," finds signs of life in Marinell's body and reports them to his mother. She, now realizing her son's immortal nature, flings away despair, as Milton's shepherd realizes Lycidas' immortal nature. Joyously she and her nymphs take him up "in their tender hands" and place his body in the "charet" and strew it with flowers. Thus, the flower-strewn vehicle is drawn by a team of dolphins to her "watry chamber" at the bottom of the sea. This bower is built

> *of hollow billowes heaped hye,*
> *Like to thicke cloudes, that threat a stormy showre,*

And vauted all within, like to the sky,
In which the Gods do dwell eternally:
There they him laid in easie couch well dight. . . .
(III.iv.43)

Spenser's comparison of this sea place to a heavenly place
and the mention of its eternal nature are suggestive of the
eternal abode of the now immortal Lycidas, who "is not
dead,/ Sunk though he be beneath the watry floar," and
who, though "sunk low," has "mounted high." In their care
of him, moreover, Cymoent and her nymphs make the reader
think of Milton's saints who care for and entertain Lycidas.
No one would suggest that in character the Nereides resemble the Christian saints, but their functions here are the
same; moreover it was almost integral to Milton's art to
transform the classical into the Christian.

Indeed, one might notice that in *Lycidas* Milton has exchanged the classical nymphs and Nereides, who had been
lax in their guardianship of the shepherd-poet, for Christian saints who are attentive. Spenser's Nereides are not
exchanged for saints, but after Marinell's overthrow they
do grow decidedly more attentive. They

> *sit all about him* [Marinell] *round,*
> *Lamenting his mishap and heauy plight;*
> *And oft his mother viewing his wide wound,*
> *Cursed the hand, that did so deadly smight*
> *Her dearest sonne, her dearest harts delight.*
> (III.iv.44)

Here one also recalls Camus' "dearest pledge."

Even after the narrative has shifted in the *Faerie Queene*
to the Guyon-Arthur story Milton seems to recall phrases
from it. In III.iv.46, Spenser's fearful damsel "with incessant
paines" suggests "with uncessant care" and the passage on

fame in *Lycidas*. But it is not until one returns to the
Marinell-Florimell story in III.viii that rather frequent
Lycidas-like phrasing as well as situations and imagery
reappear. The reopening of the story, "But *Florimell* her
selfe was farre away" (III.viii.20), will recall that Lycidas
"the shores, and sounding Seas/Wash far away." And in the
very next stanza Florimell, now in the fisherman's boat,
floated upon the calm sea:

> Long so she on the mightie maine did flote,
> And with the tide droue forward carelesslie;
> For th' aire was milde, and cleared was the skie,
> And all his windes Dan Aeolus did keepe,
> From stirring up their stormy enmity.

The passage recalls Milton's description of what followed
upon Triton's questioning the waves and the winds, and
Aeolus' (Hippotades') reply

> That not a blast was from his dungeon stray'd,
> The Ayr was calm, and on the level brine,
> Sleek Panope with all her sisters play'd.
>
> (*Lycidas* 97-99)

The imagery is essentially the same in both passages; and
the tone of the verse, alike in both, creates for us the utter
quietude so befitting the occasion.

The attack of the fisherman upon Florimell is lamented
by the formula "Where be ye now, . . ." addressed to brave
knights; but since no knight is nigh, the heavens, of

> . . . soueraine fauour towards chastity,
> Doe succour send to her distressed cace:
> So much high God doth innocence embrace.
>
> (III.viii.29)

Thus the theme found in *Comus* is introduced,[7] but more pertinent here is the echo, in the last line, of Milton's "Of so much fame in Heav'n expect thy meed."

Finally, in this passage one learns that Panope, the only one of the Nereides whom Milton names (and aside from Cymoent the only one named by Spenser up to this point) is the housekeeper of Proteus. Spenser names her again in his list of the Nereides, at the marriage of the Medway and the Thames (IV.xi.49), which story is incorporated into the latter episodes of the Marinell-Florimell narrative. This marriage ceremony contains a long and lovely procession of rivers (though Father Camus is not there) somewhat suggestive of the procession of mourners at the shepherd-poet's memorial service for Lycidas. "First came great *Neptune*, with his threeforkt mace," whose "dewy lockes did drop with brine apace," suggesting both St. Peter and Camus. But here the likeness seems to stop. The story has pretty well run its course, and its impact upon Milton seems to wane. Like Marinell, Lycidas has become, if not the guardian, then the genius of the shore; and like him, too, he has gained immortality.

The evidence of connection between *Lycidas* and the Marinell episode seems to me quite positive. There are too many similarities between the two for there to have been no connection. Spenser's narrative was part of Milton's in-

---

7. In fact, there are several resemblances to *Comus* in this passage—as one might well expect. Not only chastity's being its own protection, but the similarity of the shape-shifting Proteus to the transformations in *Comus* and the general similarity of Proteus the lecher to Comus the libertine are notable. One would not wish to claim this passage, however, as a direct source for *Comus*. See A. S. P. Woodhouse's illuminating articles, "The Argument of *Comus*," *UTQ*, XI (1941), 60, n. 13, and "Comus Once More," *UTQ*, XIX (1950), 221. Milton, unlike Spenser, seeks "to transform chastity into a positive virtue, a principle of action, not in nature, but in grace." Professor Woodhouse agrees, of course, that Sabrina comes from Spenser, and concludes that whatever else *Comus* may be, it is certainly a Spenserian allegory.

tellectual frame of reference. Having read a story so striking for its narrative (not to speak of its moral implications) and its sharply realized and unusual imagery (especially such pictures as the sea chambers at the bottom of the world, the nymphs functioning as saints, the team of dolphins, and the still ocean on which the nymphs might play), Milton's retentive memory brought its details to him at need—perhaps not consciously, very possibly not with deliberation. (In later life his imagination was "milked" each morning.) When he came to write the elegy for the drowned youth, his friend, there was deep in the chaos of his consciousness, far back in his memory, the sea story of the lamented Marinell. Out of this unshaped material, phrase, name, cadence, and image emerge, not as copied direct from Spenser, but as if suggested by his phrases, names, and images; as if they had risen from deep in the mind of Milton as he wrote. And the original impression made by Spenser seems to lie there, imbedded in the poem as in the poet's mind, enriching what makes its way, as it were, to the surface. The creative imagination, bringing order to its subject from the material of a vast mind, has apparently adapted, modified, reinterpreted, compressed and yet sharpened its subject. The larger body of intellectual substance shows through, emerges from the depths, like great boulders briefly showing through breaking waves, to give the poem much of its effect of compression. Such lines as "And, O ye *Dolphins*, waft the haples youth" reduce to a miniature the full picture from Spenser (with further possible suggestions from such other places as Ovid's *Metamorphoses* or Pausanias or even Aulus Gellius or Herodotus), as if the poet would have the reader recall by suggestion only the complete and elaborate image or images from the source or several sources.

Here is no composition *ex nihilo*, but out of a richness of mind as great as the richness of the seas themselves. Out of such richness come the restraint and compression that give power to the poem. For the poet must have much to bring order into if he is to create greatly. Lying back of *Lycidas* somewhere, perhaps not too deep in the sea caves of Milton's mind, is, I believe, Spenser's story of Marinell and Florimell, especially the first part of it. By reading it along with the elegy, one realizes more readily than one otherwise could what is compacted here, how great the compression and the suggestion, and how effectively they are accomplished.

LALIA PHIPPS BOONE

The Language of Book VI, Paradise Lost

ACCORDING TO Professor Ants Oras,[1] the critical dictum that Milton's language is both alien and archaic was well established in the eighteenth century. The main feature of Hume's *Annotations on Milton's Paradise Lost* (1695) is the explanation of Milton's obsolete words and his Latinisms, Greekisms, and Italianisms. The J. Richardsons (father and son), in their *Explanatory Notes and Remarks on Milton's Paradise Lost* (1734), praise Milton's "Pure Latinisms," examine his use of older words, and note his Italian borrowings. Thomas Newton, *Paradise Lost: A New Edition* (1749), expresses dislike for Milton's archaisms, but praises his "uncommon expressions" borrowed from classical antiquity. Thomas Warton in *Poems upon Several Occasions, English, Italian, and Latin, with Translations* (1785), explains Milton's obsolete diction in great detail. Henry John Todd, in the preface to his 1801 edition of Milton, notes his use of both archaic and Italian words.

Eighteenth-century criticism not treated by Professor Oras reflects the same trend of thought. In 1712 Addison wrote that Milton had "infused a great many Latinisms" into English and had employed "several old words" (*Spectator*, 285). Leonard Welstead described Milton's language as an "uncouth unnatural jargon ... which is a second Babel or con-

<hr/>

1. *Milton's Editors and Commentators from Patrick Hume to Henry John Todd* (Oxford, 1931), *passim*.

fusion of all languages."[2] Later, though praising certain qualities of Milton's style, Dr. Samuel Johnson borrowed critical phrases from Jonson and Butler to use in his criticism of Milton, who he said "wrote no language" but a "Babylonish dialect," labeling it a "deformity."[3]

The modern criticism that Milton's vocabulary is both alien, particularly Latin, and archaic[4] seems to be derived from these early criticisms, not from systematic analysis. For example, T. S. Eliot, taking his cue from Johnson's censure of Milton, says, "This criticism seems to be substantially true: indeed unless we accept it, I do not think we are in the way to appreciate the peculiar greatness of Milton. . . . Every distortion of construction, the foreign idiom, the use of a word in a foreign way or with the meaning of the foreign word from which it is derived rather than the accepted meaning in English, every idiosyncrasy is a particular act of violence which Milton has been the first to commit."[5] And Ezra Pound says, "Milton got into a mess trying to write English as if it were Latin."[6]

The first to attempt an analysis of Milton's language was George P. Marsh, who established an excellent precedent in method. His findings partially refute the popular opinion concerning the native content of Milton's vocabulary. He records 33 per cent native content for his total vocabulary "at rest," i.e., counting each word only once regardless of the number of times it appears; but 90 per cent native con-

---

2. *Dissertation concerning the Perfection of the English Language*, 1724 (*Works*, 1787, p. 123), as quoted by R. M. Lumiansky, "Milton's English Again," *MLN*, LV (1940), 591.
3. *Lives of the Poets*, G. B. Hill, (Oxford, 1905), I, 190-191.
4. J. H. Hanford, *A Milton Handbook*, 4th ed. (New York, 1946), pp. 293-294, despite the recognition it gives to Marsh's analysis of Milton's vocabulary, describes Milton's vocabulary as archaic and Latin. See also R. D. Havens, *The Influence of Milton on English Poetry* (Cambridge, 1922), pp. 64 and 83-84.
5. *Milton*, Annual Lecture on a Master Mind (London, 1947), p. 9.
6. *Polite Essays* (Norfolk, Conn., 1940), p. 192.

tent for *L'Allegro*, 83 per cent for *Il Penseroso*, and 80 per cent for *Paradise Lost* VI "in action," i.e., counting each George Coffin Taylor[8] and R. M. Lumiansky[9] in analyses word every time it is used.[7] Subsequent investigations by of *Lycidas* and *L'Allegro*, respectively, show that the language in these poems is predominantly native no matter what method of investigation is used. Joshua H. Neumann, in a study of Milton's prose, finds that the Anglo-Saxon element is much greater than the Latin element and that "there are very few archaisms and obsolete terms"; he concludes that Milton's linguistic innovations should "entitle him to consideration as one of the enrichers of the English language."[10]

The general purpose of this study is to build on the efforts of Taylor, Lumiansky, and Neumann, and incidentally to correct the errors of Marsh. The specific purpose is threefold: first, to find out how much of the language of *PL* VI is native; second, to determine further how much of the language is archaic; and third, to illustrate a practical methodology for linguistic analysis.

The *Oxford English Dictionary* serves as the sole authority.[11] The etymology of each word in the poem has been examined to determine, first, its ultimate origin; second, the date it entered the English language; third, the first date of its use in the same sense and form as that used by Milton in *PL* VI; and fourth, if possible, whether it was archaic at the time Milton used it. In order to make the analysis more valuable, the methods used by Marsh, Taylor, and

---

7. *Lectures on the English Language*, 6th ed., Lecture VI (New York, 1872), pp. 88-95.

8. "Milton's English," *Notes and Queries*, CLXXVIII (1940), 56-57.

9. "Milton's English Again," *MLN*, LV (1940), 591-594.

10. "Milton's Prose Vocabulary," *PMLA*, LX (1945), 102-120.

11. Scholars are aware of the limitations of the *OED*. However, despite its errors and shortcomings, it is still the best tool available for dating; I therefore use its dates in the absence of a better tool.

Lumiansky have been followed in determining the native content. The vocabulary has been examined both "in action" and "at rest."[12] Each examination is twofold: the first analysis is based on a complete vocabulary; the second, on one from which proper names, prepositions, conjunctions, and articles are excluded.

The following facts are the result of an analysis of the language "in action." Out of a total count of 6,769 words, 74.3 per cent are ultimately native, 18 per cent Latin (14.5 per cent through French), 4.1 per cent French, and 3.6 per cent all other sources.[13] When 41 proper nouns, 263 articles, 477 conjunctions, and 919 prepositions are omitted, the percentage of native content drops to 66.3 per cent with a corresponding increase of Latin content to 24.1 per cent and French to 5.5 per cent.

An analysis of the language "at rest" reveals that out of 1,842 words, 41.6 per cent are ultimately native, 39.2 per cent Latin, 11.7 per cent French, and 7.5 per cent all other sources. When 18 proper nouns, 3 articles, 10 conjunctions, and 34 prepositions are omitted, 40.3 per cent are ultimately native, 40.4 per cent Latin, 12 per cent French, and 7.3 per cent all other sources. All but 177 of the 1,842 words were in the language in some form before 1500, and three of the 177—*bickering, clashing,* and *drizzling*—are of English origin.

12. In counting the words "at rest," the following method was adhered to: (a) A word used as two parts of speech counts as two words. (b) Each word and all its inflected forms count as one word; e.g., *shall* and *should; fight, fought,* and *foughten; man* and *men; Almighty* and *Almighty's; this* and *these; high, higher,* and *highest; more* and *most;* (c) Exceptions to the practice set forth in (b): *am, was,* and *were* are counted separately, but *be* and *been* as one; *Seraph* and *Seraphim* are counted separately, since complete information is given in the *OED* under both entries.

13. Mr. Taylor says in his analysis of *Lycidas* that Marsh's results "need to be rechecked carefully." My 74.3% for the native content of *PL* VI and Lumiansky's 80% for *L'Allegro* seem to verify his judgment. However, I believe the differences in percentages are principally the result of using different lexicographical tools (Marsh does not name his sources).

Therefore, if "native" is used in the same sense that Taylor used it, little more than 9 per cent of the words used in *PL* VI are of foreign origin.[14]

A closer examination of the ultimately Latin words will, I believe, show that the Latinity of Milton's language has been overestimated. It may be that the usual reference to Milton's Latinity loosely includes syntax as well as vocabulary (as in Pound's statement above), but here I am concerned only with vocabulary. Further examination of the analysis "at rest" reveals that of the 1,842 words, 39.2 per cent are ultimately Latin. Still, only 10.1 per cent entered the language directly; the remaining 29.1 per cent were introduced by way of French. If the 29.1 per cent is added to the 11.7 per cent of ultimate French origin, 40.8 per cent of the words "at rest" are at least partially affected by French; the claim for Latin is slightly less impressive.

When one attempts to determine whether a word was

---

14. The 174 words of foreign origin entering the language after 1500 are: *acclamation, admir'd, adusted, advanc't, alt, ambient, ambiguous, ambrosial, ample, anarchy, annihilate, applauded, askance, assert, astonisht, atheist, attack, basis, battalion, careering, circumfused, combat, compare, compute, concocted, confines, conscious, conspicuous, consulting, contend, contest, contiguous, continent, contraction, convince, convolv'd, cubic, derided, dire, discontinuous, displode, dissipation, divisible, effulgence, embowell'd, enginry, eternize, ethereal, ethereous, evaded, exhausted, expect, expectation, explores, extravagant, files, fluid, globe, grateful, gross, halleluiahs, heroic, horrid, ignominious, ignominy, imitation, immediate, imminent, impal'd, imperious, impious, implacable, impure, incapable, incessant, indecent, indissolubly, inextinguishable, infuriate, insensate, instilled, instinct, intercept, interposed, interview, intestine, inventor, inviolable, invulnerable, irresistible, jaculation, jarring, liable, march* (n.), *march* (v.), *measuring, military, mineral, Moloch, myriads, nectarous, nitrous, numerous, obdur'd, obscur'd, omnipotence, omniscient, opposition, orb, orbed, orifice, paternal, pernicious, phalanx, posture, precipitates, prevalent, procinct, prodigious, promontories, proposals, propound, race, rallied, ranks* (n.), *ranks* (v.), *rapid, refulgent, reluctant, repulse, retir'd, revolt* (n.), *revolt* (v.), *rigid, rout, ruining, scouts, secure, securely, sense, separate, serried, severe, shock, silent, situate, solid, squadrons, strict, sublime, success, sulphurous, supreme, surface, Tartarus, tire, transact, transgress, unanimous, unexpected, unguarded, uninvited, unobnoxious, urg'd, Urim, vagaries, valid, variety, various, vast* (adj.), *vast* (n.), *vent, vicissitude,* and *volleys.*

archaic at a particular time, he meets many unexpected and almost insurmountable difficulties. In the first place, how long must a word be out of general use before it is considered archaic? Can its form, for example the syllabic -*ed* of *learned* or *beloved,* possibly be a clue? Is the fact that its last use is recorded, say, in 1666 indicative of archaism in 1667? Or does the failure to list subsequent usage indicate simply that its use did not change? I do not know the answers. But, if failure to record usage after 1667 is indicative of archaism in 1667, then only two of the 1,842 words "at rest" can be considered archaic. These are *present,* used adverbially, recorded last in 1654 and *presume(d), meaning* to pretend, in 1652.

A better approach to the question might be a further examination of the general characteristics of the language. Of the 1,665 words in the language in 1500, 268 underwent conversion, derivational change, or semasiological change before 1667. Those undergoing conversion are:

(1) from verb to noun: *broils, dawn, dispraise, disturb, frown, glimpse, hiss, parle, result, revenge;*
(2) from noun to verb: *hymn(ing), gain, lop(t), place(d), root, share(d), style, throng;*
(3) from adjective to noun: *festival, omnipotent, terrene, vanquisht* (substantive use of participle);
(4) from noun to adjective: *dismal, intent;*
(5) from adjective to adverb: *tenfold;*
(6) from verbal to adjective: *spread;*
(7) from verbal to noun: *content(s);*
(8) from adverb to adjective: *headlong;*
(9) from adjective to verb: *affright(ed);*
(10) from intransitive verb to transitive verb: *glared;*
(11) *gash* (from *garse* by analogy with *slash*).

Words in the English language before 1500 undergoing

derivational change between 1500 and 1667 may be divided into five groups:

(1) participles used as attributive adjectives: from verbs—*afflicted, amused, chained, compos'd, contemned, contented, crusht, disordered, forc't, foreseen, fraught, impos'd, incens't, inflam'd, languisht, redoubled, scorcht, scorned, seated, shattered, stored, aspiring, circling, conflicting, encount'ring, griding, madding, minist'ring, reflecting, straight'ning, vaunting;* from verbs entering the language after 1500, but derived from nouns in the language before 1500—*barb'd, disburden'd, overpower'd,* and *neighboring;* from verbs, the roots of which were in the language before 1500—*enlightened, inlaid, infix'd, collected* (ppl. a., from verb *collect* from pp. *collect,* which entered the language before 1500).

(2) compounds formed by combining two distinct words: *deep-throated, eagle-winged, eye-witness, four-visaged, light-armed, sun-bright, three-bolted, thunderstruck, triple-mounted, triple-row, vain-glorious, voutsafe, whirl-wind;* adverb-verb—*overwearied, over-ruled, uprooted, upstayed, uptore;* adverb-noun—*inroad, uproar.*[15]

(3) compounds formed by adding prefixes to older root words: *disappeared, encamping* (*camp,* n.), *illaudable, imbodied, impassive, imperishable* (*perishably,* from *perish,* v.), *partake, reimbattl'd, repine, unaided, unbecoming, uncreated, unconquerable, undismayed, unequal, unmixt, unnamed, unopposed, unsafe, unsound.*

(4) compounds formed by adding suffixes: *amazement* (*amaze*), *aspirer* (*aspire,* v.), *blasphemous* (*blaspheme,* adj.), *cherubic* (*cherub,* n.), *composure* (*compose*),

---

15. Mr. Bernard Groom ("The Formation and Use of Compound Epithets in English Poetry from 1579," *SPE,* V, 305) ranks Milton with Shakespeare and Spenser as one of the greatest creators of compound epithets in the English language.

divinely (*divine*, adj.), *dusky* (*dusk*, n.), *empyrean* (*empyreal*), *enjoyment* (*enjoy*), *envier* (*envy*), *gloomy* (*gloom*, n. from *gloom*, v.), *hapless* and *hapiness* (*hap*, n.) *haughty*, adj. (*haught*, adj.), *humbl'd* (*humble*, adj.), *insensibly* (*insensible*), *invincibly* (*invincible*), *matchless* (*match*), *orderly* (*order*, n.), *prevention* (*prevent*, v.), *rocky* (*rock*, n.), *satanic* (*satan*, n.), *servility* (*servile*, n.), *shaggy* (*shag*, n.), *show'ry* (*shower*), *spiritless* and *spiritous* (*spirit*), *wasteful* (*waste*).

(5) clipped words and back formations: *amaze*, n. (*amazement*, n. from *amaze*, v.); *bound*, adj. (*bounded*, adj.); *condense*, adj. (*condensed*, adj.); *seraph*, singular n. (*seraphim*, plural n.); *twixt* (*atwixt*); *van* (*vanguard*).

As is usually the case, almost half the words undergoing any change at all fall in the semasiological category. These include *assessor, breach, calmest, cancelled, cause, changed, charge, chariots, chief, circumference, circumspection, civil, combination, command, compar'd, compel, confidence, constellations, consultation, contradiction, declare, deformed, direct, discharge, discontinuous, disgorging, disputes, dissent, distinct, divides, dolorous, erroneous, fablest, filial, firm, flank, flashing, foil'd, forcible, glut, gorgeous, grand, hail, hosanna, immense, impediment, impenetrably, implements, incentive, inducive, ineffably, infernal, injury, instrumental, invaded, invent, invention, jubilee, liquid, loos'ning, merited, mixt, mould, multitudes, nameless, nativity, nicest, nimble, odds, oppose, opposite, overture, please, plotting, plumes, prefer, presented, pretense, prime, raged, reason, rebuke, reclaim, recoil'd, relate, relent, reli'd, remote, render, resistance, resolution, rest* (n.), *revive, rid, ruinous, rules* (v.), *scale, secret, serve, shrin'd, smil'd, soaring, solitary, sparkle, superior, surprised* (v.), *surveys, suspend, synod, terror, texture, touch* (n.), *tract, triumph, turns* (by turns), *undaunted, valour, vaulted, veil, veins, verge,* and *view*.

What is, perhaps, most significant is the fact that Milton is in *PL* VI responsible for 66 of these semasiological innovations. The *Oxford English Dictionary* credits him with the following 59 (words prefixed by an asterisk are used in *PL* VI in the same sense given; however, the illustrative quotation given in *OED* is taken from another portion of *PL* or, in the case of *Hosanna*, from *Church Government* II.iii, 1641 [Columbia ed., III, 252]):

*ambrosial (divinely fragrant)
approved (as an adjective)
assessor (one who sits beside a chief judge)
atheist (as an adjective)
attack (an assault)
bickering (coruscating, flashing, quivering)
calmest (of conditions or circumstances)
circumference (put for the whole circle rather than the line encompassing anything of round form)
*composure (composed condition)
*compute (to make up, count)
convolv'd (used in passive sense: to be contorted or twisted about)
defensive (of persons: capable of making defence)
discontinuous (separating continuity of parts)
displode (explode, fire)
*effulgence (quality of being effulgent)
*empyrean (the highest in heaven)
*enginry (artillery)
*ethereal (heavenly)
ethereous (composed of, of the nature of, ether)
exhausted (having one's strength and energy used up)
filial (bearing the character or relation of a son or daughter)
fourfold-visaged (as a compound)
glar'd (as a transitive verb: to send forth a glare)

glut (in the figurative sense)

griding (adjective derived from the verb *gride*)

⁕Hosanna (a cry or shout of hosanna)

hymning (as a verb from the noun *hymn*)

impassive (not subject to passion or painful sensation)

incentive (a Latinism meaning "kindling")

infuriate (as an adjective: excited to fury)

⁕instinct (as an adjective: impelled, moved, excited)

light-armed (as a compound)

loos'ning (weakening the adhesion)

⁕measuring (estimating the amount, duration, and value of an immaterial thing by comparison with some standard)

⁕Moloch (name of a Canaanite idol; represented as one of the devils)

mould (substance)

⁕nectarous (resembling nectar)

⁕opposite (in an opposite position)

⁕opposition (facing, fronting)

⁕overpow'r'd (crushed)

paternal (that which belongs to a father)

...... (of or belonging to one's father)

rallied (concentrated or revived by a strong effort of the will)

reimbattl'd (prefix *re-:* drawn up in battle array)

reluctant (of things)

⁕........ (struggling, i.e., through the smoke)

satanic (pertaining to Satan)

⁕separate (withdrawn from others)

⁕seraph (back formation of the plural *seraphim*)

⁕serried (pressed close together)

show'ry (created from the noun *shower*)

⁕soaring (transferred to any object that flies through the air)

Supreme (as a title of God)

terrene (as a noun)

three-bolted (as a compound)
unaided (prefix *un-*)
*unconquerable (of mind, feeling, etc.)
vaulted (of things: to form a vault over something)
vent (the hole or channel in the breech of a cannon or firearm through which fire is communicated to the charge; the touchhole)

The other seven innovations, although recorded by *OED* at a later date, were used by Milton in *PL* VI. They are:

careering (used in figurative sense of moving swiftly over), 1830
deep-throated (as a compound), 1884
direct (of rays), 1706
eagle-winged (as a compound), 1675
impure (adjective used substantively), 1784
presented (pointed, directed, or turned to face something), 1793
various (of war: marked by varying success), 1754-1758

It is obvious that the language of *PL* VI is not static as an archaic language would be. The 445 words showing linguistic change between 1500 and 1667 offer much more evidence that the language is living. Moreover, Milton's neologisms are sufficient to label him a linguistic innovator.

I doubt seriously that a comparison of "native lines" to "foreign lines" is fruitful in determining the relative importance of the two elements in Milton's language. Nevertheless, it has some interest. There are 51 passages containing no foreign element. These are lines 11, 59, 98, 112, 131, 137, 159, 163, 221, 274, 295, 297, 316, 341, 350, 359, 402, 417, 460, 477, 491, 500, 539, 544, 547, 559, 574, 592-594, 625-627, 648, 659, 663, 666, 669, 671, 689, 710, 724, 729, 731-732, 734, 754, 768, 779, 820, 832, 835-836, 839-840, 850, 853, and 892. Some examples are:

Hence then, and evil go with thee along
Thy offspring. . . .[16]

That whom they hit, none on their feet might stand,
Though standing else as Rocks, but down they fell
By thousands. . . .[17]

Not understood, this gift they have besides,
They show us when our foes walk not upright.[18]

   . . . when in the end
Thou shalt be All in All, and I in thee
For ever, and in mee all whom thou lov'st. . . .[19]

On the other hand, there is not a single line containing words of foreign origin only. The following contain only articles, prepositions, and conjunctions of native origin: 31, 63, 201, 224, 268, 399, 422, 434, 523, 584, 587. Possibly the best example of this last group is:

   Far otherwise th' *inviolable Saints*
   In *Cubic Phalanx* firm advanc't entire,
   Invulnerable, impenetrably arm'd.[20]

My findings can be summarized as follows:
1. Whether the proper nouns, articles, conjunctions, and prepositions are included or excluded, the language "in action" is predominantly native. Moreover, if all words in the language in 1500 are to be considered native, then 90 per cent of the total vocabulary is native. However, when the language is considered "at rest," the total native element is only slightly greater than the total Latin element.

16. *PL* VI.275-276.
17. *PL* 592-594.
18. *PL* 626-627.
19. *PL* 731-733.
20. *PL* 398-400.

2. In spite of the fact that 39 per cent of the total vocabulary "at rest" is ultimately Latin, approximately three-fourths of the Latin words entered the language through French. Therefore, I believe that the native element in the language "at rest" is more important than that of any other single language, even though the vocabulary is not predominantly native.

3. A comparison with Marsh's analysis (*Lectures on the English Language,* Lecture VI, 1872, p. 88) indicates that his 33 per cent native content for Milton's vocabulary "at rest" is too low and his 80 per cent for the total vocabulary "in action" is too high. I find 41.6 per cent native content for the language "at rest" and 74.3 per cent for the language "in action."

4. A comparison with analyses of the language of *L'Allegro, Lycidas, Il Penseroso,*[21] and the prose works

---

21. By analyzing the language of *Il Penseroso* in the manner just outlined for *PL* VI, I found: (a) An analysis "in action" reveals that out of a total count of 1066 words (11 proper nouns not listed in *OED* are excluded), 80% are ultimately native, 11% Latin (8% through French), 6% French, and 3% all other sources. When 23 proper nouns, 138 prepositions, 95 conjunctions, and 70 articles are excluded, the percentage of native content drops to 72% with a corresponding increase of Latin content to 15% and French to 8%.

(b) An analysis of the language "at rest" reveals that out of 584 words (the 11 proper nouns not listed in *OED* are excluded), 66% are ultimately native, 18% Latin, 10% French, and 6% all other sources. When 21 proper nouns (including the 11 not listed in *OED*), 22 prepositions, 9 conjunctions, and 2 articles are excluded, 63% are ultimately native, 19% Latin (14% through French), 11% French, and 7% all other sources.

(c) All but 20 of the 595 words "at rest" were in the language in some form before 1500, and one of the 20—*hist,* v.—is of English origin. Therefore, if "native" is applied to all words in the vocabulary before 1500, little more than 3% of the words in *Il Penseroso* are of foreign origin.

(d) If failure to record usage of a word after 1632 is indicative of archaism, there are three archaic words in *Il Penseroso: plight,* meaning *manner,* 1581; *removed,* recorded first in 1600 and last in *L'Allegro;* and *nook,* which appears in its figurative sense only in *Il Penseroso.*

(e) Of the 574 words in the language in 1500, 114 underwent conversion, derivational change, or semasiological change.

(f) Of those words undergoing semasiological change, Milton is respon-

show that the native element in *PL* VI is less than in the minor poems and in the prose; however, it is still the basic language of *PL*.

5. There are many more linguistic innovations than there are so-called archaisms; and Milton's own contributions show that he is a linguistic innovator, not an adopter of antiquated words.

This evidence is, it seems to me, sufficient to show, first, that the Latinity of Milton's poetic language has been overestimated, and, second, that his language is living rather than archaic.

---

sible for 24 innovations. *OED* credits him with *riding* (of heavenly bodies), *swinging* (of a bell to ring), *nook* (in the figurative sense), *call* (to bring to mind), *civil-suited* (as a compound), *twilight* (as an adjective meaning dim), *pealing* (as an adjective), *starr'd* (fixed like a star in the heavens), *Cynthia* (the moon personified; used before 1632 by Spenser in "Prothalamion" (1.121) and by Jonson in *Cynthia's Revels*, as the figurative title for Queen Elizabeth), *fleecy* (created from the noun), *gloom* (as a noun), *lonely* (of things), *drear* (as a clipped form of *dreary*), *fling* (to send forth light), *dewy-feather'd* (compound), *spell* (to study), *hist* (as a verb), and *unsphere* (in a figurative sense). Five more innovations are recorded by *OED* at a later date, but were used by Milton in *Il Penseroso*. They are *hung*, used as an adjective, 1663; *massy proof*, used as a compound, 1788; *voiced*, used as an adjective, 1637; *saintly*, 1660; and *deluding*, used as an adjective, 1654.

ANTS ORAS

Milton's Blank Verse and the Chronology of His Major Poems

UCH STRENUOUS SPECULATION has been devoted in recent years to the dates of composition of Milton's poems, notably the major ones, *Paradise Lost, Paradise Regained,* and *Samson Agonistes.* The scarcity, or lack, of reliable external evidence has led a group of critics to propound theories which, if substantiated, would entirely change the traditional chronological pattern. H. F. Fletcher, for instance, remarks that both *SA* and *PR* are "likely to have been largely composed in their general outline at almost any time after 1640, and slowly brought to completion between 1650 and 1670, their date of publication."[1] W. R. Parker subjects the evidence concerning the composition of *SA* to a detailed scrutiny, concluding, though with careful reservations, that the tragedy may well have been begun in 1646 or 1647 and then worked on at intervals over a number of years.[2] Allan H. Gilbert likewise regards *SA* as early. In his book *On the Composition of Paradise Lost*[3] he, moreover, suggests a revolutionary theory with

1. *The Complete Poetical Works of John Milton,* ed. H. F. Fletcher (Boston, 1941), p. 442.
2. "The Date of Samson Agonistes," *PQ,* XXVIII (1949), 145-166. See also A. S. P. Woodhouse, "*Samson Agonistes* and Milton's Experience," *Transactions of the Royal Society of Canada,* 3rd Ser., XLIII (1949), sect. II, 157-175, where Professor Parker's theory is rejected but another relatively early date, 1660-1661, is suggested as possible.
3. Chapel Hill, 1947.

regard to the order in which the different parts of the epic were composed. In all these cases, the evidence produced is largely internal. No weighty external evidence has been brought to light by these scholars. But they have succeeded in showing that much in the generally accepted views rests on incomplete knowledge and can with some plausibility be represented as a matter of mere belief.

Among the arguments put forward in support of the re-dating of Milton's major works there are relatively few that touch on his poetical technique, not a single aspect of which has so far been consistently examined throughout his poetical output with a view to establishing the chronology of his poems. It has even been suggested that any application of stylistic or prosodical tests would be somewhat irrelevant, considering Milton's keen sense of stylistic "decorum."[4] But granting that Milton's feeling for "decorum" influenced his style, certain aspects of the latter would appear to be too deep-seated to have been radically affected by any such influences, for example, certain basic features of rhythm. While many surface phenomena may have changed, a residue of more persistent habits, preferences, and trends is likely to have survived any application of "decorum," regardless of whether what was being composed was a "diffuse epic," a "brief epic," or a tragedy in the ancient manner. A poet's conscious modification of his rhythm for specific effects would, it seems, tend to keep within the limits determined by his personal feeling for rhythm, his individual rhythmical taste. Whatever he does is liable to be influenced by this partly instinctive total attitude. Even while experimenting and deliberately exploring new rhythmical possibilities, he will hardly abandon his old habits at once, particularly if he continues to use the same meter: the new devices will have to be incorporated into the existing pattern. So, the total configuration of rhythmical trends will seldom undergo

4. Parker, 155.

any sudden radical changes, except, perhaps, for instance, after an interval of poetical unproductivity sufficiently prolonged to weaken or break the associations with the poet's earlier practice, or after a period of profound mental upheaval, which may conceivably produce a similar effect. A possibility that also comes to mind is an author's deliberate attempt to suppress his rhythmical individuality for the purposes of a pastiche or a verse translation. Yet even pastiches and translations have a notorious tendency to betray their authors' identity. It is difficult to think of any long piece of work of this kind in the English language by a writer otherwise possessed of a genuine rhythm of his own which would suggest any real rhythmical self-effacement. A personal rhythm seems easy to efface only when it is weakly developed or nonexistent.

In a statistical inquiry the basic rhythmical pattern of the period can, of course, emerge distinctly only if a sufficient body of verse is available for examination. Thus, a single scene of a blank verse play would hardly reveal it distinctly, but an act or two might, and an entire play usually would. A study of the metrical data on Shakespeare assembled by Sir E. K. Chambers[5] shows clearly, I think, that Shakespeare's metrical patterns are determined by the period rather than the genre. This becomes especially apparent if we translate Chambers' figures into percentages where he has not done so himself. Most of the figures for the plays of Shakespeare's fourth period, for instance, will then be found to be surprisingly alike, irrespective of the genre. Thus, *Coriolanus* is in most respects much closer to *Cymbeline*, *The Winter's Tale*, or *The Tempest* than to *Hamlet* or *Julius Caesar*. *Hamlet*, in its turn, is very like *Twelfth Night*, and *Julius Caesar* like *Much Ado About Nothing*. *All's Well That Ends Well*, although a comedy, resembles *Othello*, *King Lear*, and *Macbeth* rather than *Twelfth Night*, *Much Ado*, or *As You*

5. *William Shakespeare: A Study of Facts and Problems*, II, 397 ff.

Like It. And so on. My own as yet unpublished inquiries into the distribution of pauses over the verse line in Shakespeare and other Elizabethan and Jacobean dramatists seem to indicate even more emphatically at least in this specific respect that the genre counts for little, whereas the period pattern is as a rule fairly clearly discernible. The line of development, though often sinuous, on the whole suggests only a gradual process of change.

Different prosodical devices naturally tend to be used with varying degrees of deliberateness. The more instinctive such a device, the less likely it is to be affected by "decorum." "Probably the variations that most easily become unconscious are those of pausation," says Chambers,[6] and there seems to be every reason to agree with him, especially as regards the parts of the line on which the pauses fall. It is at any rate difficult to think of any considerations of genre that might cause a writer, for instance, to prefer pauses in the first half of lines to such in the second half, or vice versa. An analogous case is the position of polysyllables in the verse. The extent to which a poet resorts to a polysyllabic diction may be decisively influenced by the genre of his composition. Thus, a lively comedy would normally call for a more sparing use of long, rolling polysyllables than a tragedy or an epic. But the metrical positions of such expressions preferred by the writer are much less likely to be influenced by the genre. Any continuity of development discovered with regard to such preferences would probably to a considerable degree reflect the gradually changing basic rhythmical attitude of the author.

In certain other respects it is perhaps possible to assume a more "genre-conscious" attitude on the author's part. It is, for example, probable that Milton considered feminine endings less suitable for epic than for dramatic compositions, since he uses them much less frequently in his two

6. *Ibid.*, I, 268.

epics than in *Comus* or in *SA*. In a case like this, evidence of changing practice within the limits of one genre and comparison with possible parallel changes in the other genre may still provide us with chronological clues. Does Milton's practice with regard to feminine endings in the epic poems seem to throw any light on the order of composition of these poems and their parts? If it does, do we find the line of development to lead us nearer *SA* or away from it? At what point does Milton's use of feminine endings in the epics most closely resemble his usage in *SA*? Do we discover any differences between *Comus* and *SA* corresponding to the differences between those parts of his epics which seem to have been composed first and those which our inquiries have led us to regard as late?

It is against the background of such considerations and queries that an attempt will be made in the following pages to trace a number of aspects of Milton's blank verse from *Comus* to *SA*. The primary object of this study is not aesthetic analysis but chronology: Milton's metrical practice will be dealt with in regard to its bearing on chronological problems. A fuller analysis of its artistic implications must be postponed. It goes without saying that any chronological conclusions which may be reached can apply only to Milton's text as it stands. It will be difficult or impossible to determine the extent to which earlier drafts may have been incorporated in the final texts, since Milton's habits of revision seem to have been too thorough and his recastings too homogeneous to leave many telltale traces. That he knew how to blend his materials seems to be clearly proved by the way he utilized parts of the passages of *Comus* cancelled in the Trinity College manuscript.[7]

7. See also Gilbert, *On the Composition of Paradise Lost*, pp. 157-159. Professor Gilbert considers it improbable that any early passages used by Milton should have failed to be "revised and adapted to their new surroundings," especially if, as is most likely, they "were taken not from paper but from the poet's memory."

In the present study Milton's poems and their parts will be examined in the usual order, so as to ascertain whether the emerging patterns agree or conflict with the traditional chronology. In order to facilitate comparison, the statistical tables, while giving the figures for each book of *PL*, also supply the totals for the two halves of the poem, Books I-VI and Books VII-XII, which are nearly equal in length. The text to which the references are made is that of H. C. Beeching's Oxford edition, but it has been checked with H. F. Fletcher's facsimile edition.* In counting the number of lines, the insertions made in the second edition of *PL* have been disregarded. Since this study is confined to Milton's blank verse, the figures do not include the songs or tetrameters in *Comus* or the lyrical passages in *SA*. The short lines of the tragedy have also been left out of account.

While all the following sections rest on a statistical basis, the method of approach varies according to the material. Sections I and II, dealing with Milton's treatment of strong pauses and polysyllables, will be found to be much more heavily statistical than the others. It seemed regrettable, but in this case unfortunately logical, to have to place the driest evidence first. The rest of this paper (which should have its independent evidential value) has been so presented as to make it possible to read it separately with a minimum of loss.

I

TREATMENT OF STRONG PAUSES

In the present section an attempt will be made to examine Milton's treatment of strong pauses, that is, for our purposes, pauses indicated in the first edition by punctuation marks

---

* Miss Helen Darbishire's excellent edition of Milton, being incomplete, could hardly be used for comparative statistics. An examination of several books of *PL* produced relative figures usually differing from mine only by a few decimal points.

stronger than a comma.[8] Table 1 gives for *Comus, PL, PR,* and *SA:*

(1) the number of strong pauses found at line endings (terminal pauses)

(2) the number of such pauses found inside lines (medial pauses)

(3) the percentage of terminal pauses in the total number of strong pauses

(4) the percentage of terminal pauses

(5) the number of strong pauses of both kinds and their frequency per 1000 lines

TABLE 1
STRONG PAUSES

	Absolute figures & per cent Terminal pauses	Medial pauses	Totals of strong pauses	Strong pauses per 1000 lines	No. of lines
Comus	155 (69.5%)	68 (30.5%)	223	281.6	792
PL I	100 (41.2%)	143 (58.8%)	243	304.5	798
II	143 (37.3%)	240 (62.7%)	383	363.0	1055
III	140 (63.6%)	80 (36.4%)	220	296.5	742
IV	194 (52.6%)	175 (47.4%)	369	363.5	1015
V	155 (49.8%)	156 (50.2%)	311	344.0	904
VI	143 (45.5%)	171 (54.5%)	314	344.3	912
I-VI	875 (47.6%)	965 (52.4%)	1840	339.1	5426
VII	104 (47.5%)	115 (52.5%)	219	342.2	640
VIII	138 (56.8%)	105 (43.2%)	243	374.4	649
IX	252 (61.3%)	159 (38.7%)	411	345.6	1189
X	158 (43.5%)	205 (56.5%)	363	328.8	1104
XI	174 (51.6%)	163 (48.4%)	337	375.7	897
XII	109 (47.8%)	119 (52.2%)	228	354.0	644
VII-XII	935 (51.9%)	866 (48.1%)	1801	351.5	5123
I-XII	1810 (49.7%)	1831 (50.3%)	3641	344.2	10549
PR I	104 (63.8%)	59 (36.2%)	163	324.7	502
II	115 (66.9%)	57 (33.1%)	172	353.9	486
III	111 (66.1%)	57 (33.9%)	168	379.2	443
IV	137 (64.6%)	75 (35.4%)	212	331.8	639
I-IV	467 (65.3%)	248 (34.7%)	715	345.4	2070
SA	381 (69.5%)	167 (30.5%)	548	409.6	1338

8. During his blindness Milton is likely to have supervised the use of the stronger and more important punctuation marks with greater strictness

This table shows *Comus* to have the fewest strong pauses per 1000 lines, but the figures for *PL* I and III are nearly as low. Indeed, at first the frequencies in *PL* move up and down rather abruptly, almost as if the poet were still experimenting. From Book IV onwards the general level in *PL* is noticeably higher, and the contrasts, though appreciable, are less marked. The greatest difference after Book IV, that between Books X and XI (46.9 per mill), is exceeded by the differences between Books I and II (58.5) and Books III and IV (67.0). *PR*, while beginning with a relatively low frequency close to that for *PL* X, thereupon shows a steady upward trend through the first three books. The deep drop in the last book makes its average fall below the aver-

---

than that of commas, which would seem to guarantee for the former a greater degree of authenticity. Moreover, pauses indicated by a mere comma, while sometimes fairly strong, only too often hardly differ in strength from such not marked by any kind of punctuation.

One point in my method of determining the position of strong pauses within the line needs perhaps to be made clear. In those cases where the pauses fall between two unstressed syllables, the first syllable is not counted. In such a line as: "Alone and helpless! Is this the confidence" (*Comus* 583) the syllable immediately before the pause is regarded as extrametrical. The analogy here is with feminine line endings. In the later works, elision and contraction (as defined by Bridges) account for the cases in question: the seemingly redundant syllable becomes, at least theoretically, nonexistent. See, e.g.: "In equal ruin: into what Pit thou seest" (*PL* X.720); or "O miserable of happie! is this the end" (*PL* X.720). In the former quotation *ruin* counts as a monosyllable; in the latter the final vowel of *happie* is, at any rate fictively, merged with the vowel of *is*. Such instances are not numerous, however, and their effect on the percentages is very slight.

For a study of some of the rhythmical implications of Milton's use of the heaviest stops, i.e., periods, colons, and their equivalents, see Theodore H. Banks, Jr., "Miltonic Rhythm: A Study of the Relation of the Full Stops to the Rhythm of *Paradise Lost*," PMLA, XLII (1927), 140-145. E. P. Morton, *The Technique of English Non-Dramatic Blank Verse* (Chicago, 1910) briefly compares Milton's treatment of pauses with that of other poets. He notes the bearing which a study of certain features of pausation might have on chronological problems.

Observations of real value on this set of problems are contained in S. E. Sprott's *Milton's Art of Prosody* (Oxford, 1953), especially in ch.IX. It is to be regretted that the delay in the publication of Sprott's long-announced book made it impossible to utilize its findings in the present paper. Sprott's statistical tables unfortunately fail to give the absolute figures on which his percentages are based.

ages of *PL* I-VI and *PL* VII-XII; but the highest figure in *PR*, that for Book III, exceeds all frequencies prior to *SA*, which forms a final culmination.

The over-all trend is towards an increased use of strong pauses. This tendency agrees with Milton's growing preference for briefer clauses and sentences: a technique of prolonged rhetorical and rhythmical suspense seems to be changing into one of more concentration in less space.

These changes may be represented graphically as follows:

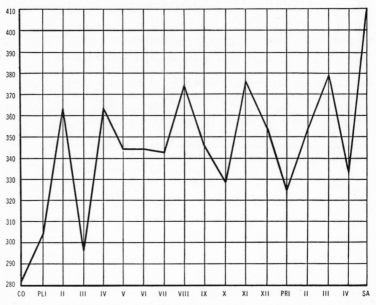

A—*Frequencies of all strong pauses (per 1000 lines)*

The line of development is somewhat different if the figures for terminal and medial pauses are compared. The percentages in the first two columns of Table 1 show early in *PL* a sharp contrast with *Comus*, but there is a marked reaction in Book III, where the percentage of medial pauses reverts to a figure only 5.9 per cent higher than in *Comus*. The figures for medial pauses then climb steadily through

Books IV, V, and VI. Then there is a gradual decline through Book IX, followed by a revival in the last three books. The downward trend started in Book VII thereupon begins again and continues more distinctly in *PR,* dropping close to the level of *Comus.* In *SA* this tendency persists and the figure is again exactly as in the early masque.

The following graph represents these trends in terms of the figures for medial pauses.

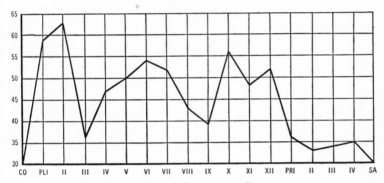

B—*Percentages of medial pauses in all strong pauses*

This decrease in the use of medial pauses suggests an easing of that complex tension between syntax and meter characteristic of so much of *PL:* the strong syntactical pauses coincide more and more frequently with the expected rest at the end of the line. Milton's verse grows quieter, its flow becomes more even, more "classical."

One would expect this tendency to be reflected in the figures for lines without any terminal punctuation, i.e., run-on lines.[9] Both run-on lines and medial pauses are devices directly opposed to a technique treating the verse line as the dominant prosodical unit. There should, then, be some

9. Run-on lines—i.e., lines with no final pause or only an extremely light one—are liable to be spotted differently by different critics. The problem is what constitutes an "extremely light" pause. To obviate this difficulty and to avoid subjectivity I permit myself to be guided by the punctuation of the first editions.

parallelism between the pattern for run-on lines and that for medial pauses. Table 2 gives (1) the number of such lines and (2), in parenthesis, their percentage in the total number of lines.

TABLE 2
RUN-ON LINES

	Absolute figures	Percentages
Comus	316	(39.9)
PL I	530	(66.4)
II	681	(64.5)
III	390	(52.6)
IV	626	(61.7)
V	548	(60.6)
VI	540	(59.2)
I-VI	3315	(61.1)
VII	389	(60.8)
VIII	336	(51.8)
IX	631	(53.1)
X	653	(59.1)
XI	504	(56.2)
XII	373	(57.9)
VII-XII	2886	(56.3)
I-XII	6201	(58.8)
PR I	262	(52.2)
II	202	(41.6)
III	194	(43.8)
IV	278	(43.5)
I-IV	936	(45.2)
SA	563	(42.1)

There is, as expected, a definite correspondence between the figures in this table and those in the previous one. The figures for lines without any terminal punctuation run approximately parallel to those for strong medial pauses and are in a roughly inverse ratio to those for strong terminal pauses. The contrast to *Comus* is most pronounced in *PL* I and then decreases, until in *SA* the figure declines almost to the level of the masque. A marked trend back towards *Comus* starts in *PL* VIII. The highest percentage in the

second half of *PL*—at the beginning of it—falls slightly below the average of the first half, while the highest percentage
in *PR*—also found at the beginning—is almost identical with
the lowest figure in *PL*. *SA* again has a percentage barely
exceeding the lowest percentage in *PR*. After *PL* VII no
figure reaches 60 per cent; after *PR* I none reaches 45 per
cent.

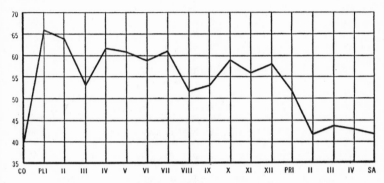

C—*Percentages of lines without any terminal punctuation*

The following two tables show the distribution of strong
pauses over the pentameter line. Table 3 gives the absolute
figures, and Table 4, the percentages in the total number of
strong medial pauses.

A comparison of the figures for *Comus*, for the first and
the second half of *PL*, for *PR*, and for *SA* reveals some
clearly marked features. The *Comus* pattern is unlike any
of the later patterns, whereas the two halves of *PL* closely
resemble each other as well as *PR*. Indeed, the divergences
between the second half of *PL* and *PR* are mostly confined
to only a few decimal points. *SA*, in its turn, differs markedly
from *PL* VII-XII and *PR* only in regard to pauses after the
sixth and seventh metrical places. *PL* I-VI seems firmly
bracketed with *PL* VII-XII, the latter even more firmly with
PR, and *SA* both with *PL* VII-XII and with *PR*.

TABLE 3

DISTRIBUTION OF STRONG MEDIAL PAUSES OVER THE PENTAMETER LINE
(Absolute figures)

	1	2	3	4	5	6	7	8	9	Totals of pauses	Total frequencies per 1000 lines
	Metrical places after which the strong medial pauses occur										
Comus	_	2	_	12	5	34	9	4	2	68	85.9
PL I	_	4	6	42	27	37	18	9	_	143	179.5
II	_	12	15	71	42	70	19	11	_	240	227.5
III	_	4	2	20	17	25	4	8	_	80	107.8
IV	1	8	12	61	22	55	7	9	_	175	172.4
V	_	3	10	42	23	52	11	15	_	156	172.6
VI	1	11	22	47	19	45	15	10	1	171	187.5
I-VI	2	42	67	283	150	284	74	62	1	965	177.8
VII	_	10	17	28	8	30	8	13	1	115	179.7
VIII	_	6	11	25	14	26	11	12	_	105	161.8
IX	1	10	16	45	18	39	20	10	_	159	133.7
X	_	10	11	47	28	66	27	16	_	205	185.7
XI	_	6	15	33	16	64	17	12	_	163	181.7
XII	_	3	8	30	23	37	12	6	_	119	184.8
VII-XII	1	45	78	208	107	262	95	69	1	866	169.0
I-XII	3	87	145	491	257	546	169	131	2	1831	173.6
PR I	_	5	5	13	7	18	3	7	1	59	117.5
II	_	1	5	13	8	18	6	5	1	57	117.3
III	_	4	6	11	7	17	9	3	_	57	128.7
IV	_	3	8	23	13	20	6	2	_	75	117.4
I-IV	_	13	24	60	35	73	24	17	2	248	119.8
SA	_	5	12	44	22	43	28	13	_	167	124.8

Certain dominant trends in Milton's way of placing his strong pauses will appear if we subject the data in Table 3 to further analysis. Milton is noted for his use of pauses in extreme positions, near the beginning and the end of lines. In Table 5, the strong pauses following the first, second, third, seventh, eighth, and ninth places, i.e., the extreme pauses, are grouped together under e (= extreme); m (= middle) indicates pauses occurring after the fourth, fifth, and sixth places—those in the middle of the line.

TABLE 4

DISTRIBUTION OF STRONG MEDIAL PAUSES OVER THE PENTAMETER LINE
(Percentages)

	1	2	3	4	5	6	7	8	9
Comus	--	2.9	--	17.6	7.4	50.0	13.2	5.9	2.9
PL I	--	2.8	4.2	29.4	18.9	25.9	12.6	6.3	--
II	--	5.0	6.2	29.6	17.5	29.1	7.9	4.6	--
III	--	5.0	2.5	25.0	21.2	31.2	5.0	10.0	--
IV	0.6	4.6	6.9	34.9	12.6	31.4	4.0	5.1	--
V	--	1.9	6.4	26.9	14.7	33.3	7.0	9.7	--
VI	0.6	6.4	12.9	27.5	11.1	26.3	8.8	5.8	0.6
I-VI	0.2	4.3	6.9	29.3	15.5	29.4	7.7	6.4	0.1
VII	--	8.7	14.8	24.3	6.9	26.1	6.9	11.3	0.9
VIII	--	5.7	10.5	23.8	13.3	24.8	10.5	11.4	--
IX	0.6	6.3	10.1	28.3	11.3	24.5	12.6	6.3	--
X	--	4.9	5.3	22.9	13.6	32.2	13.2	7.8	--
XI	--	3.7	9.2	20.2	9.8	39.3	10.4	7.4	--
XII	--	2.5	6.7	25.2	19.3	31.1	10.1	5.0	--
VII-XII	0.1	5.2	9.0	24.0	12.4	30.2	11.0	7.9	0.1
I-XII	0.2	4.7	7.9	26.8	14.0	29.8	9.2	7.1	0.1
PR I	--	8.5	8.5	22.0	11.8	30.5	5.1	11.8	1.7
II	--	1.7	8.8	22.8	14.0	31.6	10.5	8.8	1.7
III	--	7.0	10.5	19.3	12.3	29.8	15.8	5.3	--
IV	--	4.0	10.7	30.7	17.3	26.7	8.0	2.7	--
I-IV	--	5.2	9.7	24.2	14.1	29.4	9.7	6.8	0.8
SA	--	3.0	7.2	26.3	13.2	25.7	16.8	7.8	--

The percentages of *e* are low in the earlier books of *PL,*
falling even below the level of *Comus,* but they begin to
increase in *PL* V, reaching a peak in *PL* VII, whereupon
they steadily decline until the end of the poem. In the first
three books of *PR* the figures are again higher, but in *PR* IV
the percentage decreases considerably, bringing the average
for the poem somewhat below that for *PL* VII-XII. This
exceptional drop seems to be connected with the unusually
calm, controlled tone of most of *PR* IV.[10] Apart from this

10. The speeches in Book IV have only about half as many extreme
pauses per 100 lines as those of Book III, where the debate between Christ

TABLE 5
MIDDLE AND EXTREME STRONG PAUSES

	Absolute figures	Percentages
Comus	51m+17e=68	75.0m+25.0e
PL I	106m+37e=143	74.1m+25.9e
II	183m+57e=240	76.2m+23.7e
III	62m+18e=80	77.5m+22.5e
IV	138m+37e=175	78.9m+21.1e
V	117m+39e=156	75.0m+25.0e
VI	111m+60e=171	64.9m+35.1e
I-VI	717m+248e=965	74.3m+25.7e
VII	66m+49e=115	57.4m+42.6e
VIII	65m+40e=105	61.9m+38.1e
IX	102m+57e=159	64.2m+35.8e
X	141m+64e=205	68.8m+31.2e
XI	113m+50e=163	69.3m+30.7e
XII	90m+29e=119	75.6m+24.4e
VII-XII	577m+289e=866	66.6m+33.4e
I-XII	1294m+537e=1831	70.7m+29.3e
PR I	38m+21e=59	64.4m+35.6e
II	39m+18e=57	68.4m+31.6e
III	35m+22e=57	61.4m+38.6e
IV	56m+19e=75	74.7m+25.3e
I-IV	168m+80e=248	67.7m+32.3e
SA	109m+58e=167	65.3m+34.7e

one book the average for *PR* is 35.3 per cent—that is, almost the same as in *SA*.

The movement here, though decidedly undulant, leads on the whole away from *Comus*. The figures for *e* in *PL* I-V are all under 30 per cent; after *PL* V only *PL* XII and *PR* IV

---

and the Tempter is at its most animated, and considerably fewer than those of Books I and II. Except in the speeches few extreme pauses are used in any part of *PR*. Certain other features of the speeches and the narrative parts of Milton's epics suggest interesting problems, which, however, will have to be dealt with elsewhere. The data which I have collected lend strong support to the conclusions reached in the present paper. See notes 17 and 33.

fail to reach that level. But the difference between the two extreme ends of the column is not very marked; it is perceptibly exceeded by that between *Comus* and *PL* VII. A truly notable feature in this table is, however, the surprising continuity of the pattern throughout *PL*. Beginning almost exactly at the level of *Comus* the figures go at first down, then up, and then down again quite evenly, without any minor jerks or fluctuations, linking each book firmly to its predecessor.[11]

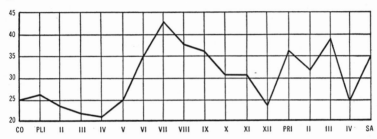

D—*Percentages of extreme strong pauses*

11. These extreme pauses often serve to intensify run-on effects when they are placed immediately before or after a run-on ending. This device is rare in *Comus,* but its incidence suddenly rises in *PL* I, and again in *PL* VI, culminating in *PL* VII; it then declines but maintains a rather even level from *PL* XII through *SA*. The figures for such combinations of enjambment with extreme strong pauses—with percentages in the totals of lines without any final punctuation placed in parenthesis—are as follows:

 Comus: 9 (2.8%).
 PL I: 34 (6.4%); II: 41 (6.0%); III: 16 (4.1%); IV: 27 (4.3%);
  V: 28 (5.1%); VI: 50 (9.3%). *PL* I-IV: 196 (5.9%).
 PL VII: 39 (10.0%); VIII: 29 (8.6%); IX: 42 (6.7%); X: 48 (7.3%);
  XI: 41 (8.2%); XII: 27 (7.2%). *PL* VII-XII: 226 (7.8%).
 PR I: 18 (6.9%); II: 13 (6.4%); III: 12 (6.2%); IV: 17 (6.1%),
  All of *PR:* 60 (6.4%).
 SA: 36 (6.4%).
Whereas in *Comus* only about half of all extreme strong pauses (52.9%) are used in run-on contexts, the proportion rises steeply in *PL*, varying from 71.8% (Book V) to 93.1% (Book XII). The average percentages are: 79.4% in *PL* I-VI, 78.2% in *PL* VII-XII, 75.0% in *PR*, and 62.0% in *SA*. *PR* III, with 63.1%—the lowest percentage between *Comus* and *SA*—anticipates the practice of the tragedy. The impression these patterns create is one of continuous development with only relatively slight fluctuation, if we except the abrupt change from *Comus* to *PL* and the changes in the middle of *PL*, both reminiscent of other statistical sequences already examined.

Much greater differences between *PR* and *SA*, on the one
hand, and *Comus* on the other hand, become apparent if
we examine the distribution of strong pauses in the earlier
and in the later part of the pentameter line. A glance at
Table 3 shows that in *Comus* the figures for the first half
of the line are exceptionally low. Its extreme strong pauses,
as well as any other strong pauses, mostly occur after the
middle of the line. In Table 6 the pauses are re-grouped
according to their position: (1) in the first half of the line
(= *a*); (2) in the exact middle, i.e., after the fifth metrical
place (= *m*); or (3) in the second half of the line (= *b*).

TABLE 6

STRONG PAUSES IN THE FIRST HALF, THE EXACT MIDDLE, AND THE
SECOND HALF OF THE LINE

	Absolute figures	Percentages
Comus	14a+5m+49b=68	20.6a+7.4m+72.0b
PL I	52a+27m+64b=143	36.4a+18.9m+44.7b
II	98a+42m+100b=240	40.8a+17.5m+41.6b
III	26a+17m+37b=80	32.5a+21.2m+46.2b
IV	82a+22m+71b=175	46.9a+12.6m+40.5b
V	55a+23m+78b=156	35.2a+14.7m+50.0b
VI	81a+19m+71b=171	47.4a+11.1m+41.5b
I-VI	394a+150m+421b=965	40.8a+15.5m+43.6b
VII	55a+8m+52b=115	47.8a+6.9m+45.2b
VIII	42a+14m+49b=105	40.0a+13.3m+46.7b
IX	72a+18m+69b=159	45.3a+11.3m+43.4b
X	68a+28m+109b=205	33.1a+13.6m+53.2b
XI	54a+16m+93b=163	33.1a+9.8m+57.1b
XII	41a+23m+55b=119	34.4a+19.3m+46.2b
VII-XII	332a+107m+427b=866	38.3a+12.4m+49.3b
I-XII	726a+257m+848b=1831	39.6a+14.0m+46.3b
PR I	23a+7m+29b=59	39.0a+11.8m+49.1b
II	19a+8m+30b=57	33.3a+14.0m+52.6b
III	21a+7m+29b=57	36.8a+12.3m+50.9b
IV	34a+13m+28b=75	45.3a+17.3m+37.3b
I-IV	97a+35m+116b=248	39.1a+14.1m+46.8b
SA	61a+22m+84b=167	36.5a+13.2m+50.3b

The one immediately obvious feature in Table 6 is the shift towards the earlier part of the line as we pass from *Comus* to *PL*. While *Comus* has three and a half times as many strong pauses in the second half of the line as in the first half, *PL* I approaches and *PL* II almost achieves a balance between the two halves.[12] Thereupon we find a zigzag movement—perhaps indicating experimentation—in Books III to VI, with the first half predominating in Books IV and VI. *PL* VII has almost exactly the same relative figure for the first half as *PL* VI, but that for the second half nearly equals it: the predominance of the first half has diminished almost to vanishing point. From then on throughout the rest of *PL* the figures for the first half of the line tend to decrease. In Books VII and IX the two halves maintain a

12. The artistic implications of this shift may perhaps be best illustrated by two passages with especially heavy internal punctuation, one from *Comus* (147-154), the other from *PL* VII (466-474):

   (a) Run to your shrouds, within these Brakes and Trees,
         Our number may affright: Som Virgin sure
         (For so I can distinguish by mine Art)
         Benighted in these Woods. Now to my charms,
         And to my wily trains, I shall e're long
         Be well stock't with as fair a herd as graz'd
         About my Mother *Circe*. Thus I hurl
         My dazling Spells into the spungy ayr....

   (b)   The Ounce,
         The Libbard, and the Tyger, as the Moale
         Rising, the crumbl'd Earth above them threw
         In Hillocks; the swift Stag from under ground
         Bore up his branching head: scarse from his mould
         Behemoth biggest born of Earth upheav'd
         His vastness: Fleec't the Flocks and bleating rose
         As Plants: ambiguous between Sea and Land
         The River Horse and scalie Crocodile.

Much of the obvious difference in the rhythm of these two passages is caused by the entirely different distribution of the pauses. In the *Comus* passage, the strong pauses are all within the second half of the line, and even of the weaker pauses only two occur within the first half. In the later passage, five main pauses appear in the first half, four of these very early in the line, after the second or third syllable. The result is a signal increase in the variety and mobility of the rhythm.

relative balance, but in the last three books the second half clearly predominates, as it also does throughout the first three books of *PR*, only Book IV constituting an exception in favor of the first half. In *SA* the second half is distinctly preferred for strong pauses, and the figures again are almost identical with the average figures for *PR* I-III ($=36.4a+12.8m+50.7b$).

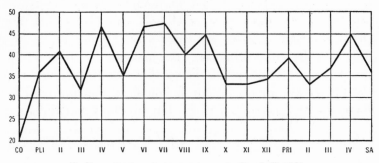

E—*Percentages of strong pauses in first half of line*

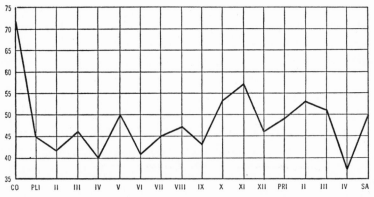

F—*Percentages of strong pauses in second half of line*

We have here a repetition of the picture of a marked change between *Comus* and the beginning of *PL*, and of a counter-movement, starting here in Book VII, running through the rest of *PL*, and continuing in *PR* and *SA*.

A study of the figures in Tables 3 and 4 reveals, however, that these results do not come about in a uniform fashion. The decrease in the relative importance of the first half of the verse in *PL* VII-XII is mainly due to a considerable drop in the figure for pauses after the fourth metrical place, while the extreme pauses at the beginning of lines have actually increased in relative weight, though not enough to restore the balance. In *PR* the relative figure for pauses after the fourth place remains almost as in *PL* VII-XII, but the frequencies of extreme pauses near the end of the line decline sufficiently to cause some change in favor of the first half. In *SA*, where the pauses after the fourth and the sixth place are almost exactly balanced, the increasing predominance of the second half is largely due to an abundant use of pauses after the seventh place. Yet while the details vary in each case and while Milton seems to be constantly trying new experiments, there remains the fact of a distinct over-all pattern. What we apparently see in the present case is an extension of Milton's area of experimentation to parts of the verse line in which he does not seem to have been very keenly interested in his early work. In the latter the attention seems to be mainly focused on the parts closest to the line endings, a feature which may be connected with the predominantly end-stopped technique of Milton in this period. As this technique is discarded, his experiments with strong pauses in the early part of the line become much more numerous; but as it gradually begins to reassert itself there is a general tendency for the frequency of such pauses to decrease.

A further point important for understanding the effect of Milton's verse is the extent to which he uses strong pauses immediately preceded by a syllable carrying a main or secondary stress or preceded by an unstressed syllable, i.e., masculine and feminine pauses. It would be equivalent to the difference between strong pauses coming after odd or even metrical places were it not for Milton's numerous metrical inversions. In examining his pauses from this angle, I had to eliminate certain indeterminate cases which did not belong clearly to either of these two categories: altogether, twenty-two instances. They are (1) pauses following words with a final vowel apparently subject to only theoretical elision (*PL* I.338, 549; II.460; VIII.556; IX.546; X.75, 86, 720, 762; XI.336; *PR* I.41; III.430); (2) pauses following words with medial elision which seems but fictive (*PL* I.90,

TABLE 7
FEMININE AND MASCULINE PAUSES
(f = fem.; m = masc.)

	Absolute figures	Percentages
Comus	27f+41m	39.7f+60.3m
PL I	53f+86m	38.1f+61.9m
II	75f+163m	31.5f+68.5m
III	23f+56m	29.1f+70.9m
IV	42f+133m	24.0f+76.0m
V	42f+114m	26.9f+73.1m
VI	59f+111m	34.7f+65.3m
I-VI	294f+663m	30.7f+69.3m
VII	33f+82m	28.7f+71.3m
VIII	37f+65m	36.2f+63.7m
IX	55f+102m	35.0f+65.0m
X	65f+135m	32.5f+67.5m
XI	47f+115m	29.0f+71.0m
XII	42f+77m	35.3f+64.7m
VII-XII	279f+576m	32.6f+67.4m
I-XII	573f+1239m	31.6f+68.4m
PR I	16f+42m	27.6f+72.4m
II	18f+39m	31.6f+68.4m
III	22f+34m	39.3f+60.7m
IV	26f+48m	35.1f+64.9m
I-IV	82f+163m	33.5f+66.5m
SA	63f+104m	37.7f+62.3m

318; VI.205; X.200; *PR* IV.624); (3) two cases where it does not seem clear where the stress is intended to fall (*PL* VIII.

57, 271); (4) *PL* IX.904, where the elision of the third vowel in *forbidd'n* seems open to doubt; (5) *PL* III.108, where it may seem questionable which of two cases of the word *reason* is subjected to elision.

Milton's preference for the more emphatic masculine pauses grows after *Comus,* but not suddenly. *PL* I has a figure for *m* very similar to that of *Comus.* A distinct, and increasing, difference from *Comus* is observable from *PL* II onwards, but in the middle of the poem, in Book VI, a marked change begins which brings the percentages considerably closer to the masque. Only three times after *PL* VI —in *PL* VII and XI and in *PR* I—does the figure for *f* fall below 30 per cent. The percentages for *PL* I-VI, VII-XII, *PR,* and *SA* show a continuous movement back towards *Comus.*

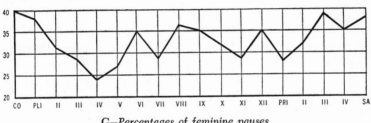

G—*Percentages of feminine pauses*

To sum up our principal results: the statistical data, despite some inevitable fluctuation, show a remarkable degree of continuity. This seems most naturally explained if we assume, in the main, a similar continuity in the order of composition. Moreover, the pattern, while revealing minor differences as we approach the pauses from various angles, remains usually the same in its salient features. There is as a rule in the first half of *PL* a contrast with *Comus*—often very sharp—the most important instances of which are perhaps the greatly intensified use of strong pauses in the first half of the pentameter line and the pronounced increase in the frequency of lines without any final punctuation. These, as well as most of the other tendencies contrasting with *Comus* that have been noted, subside then to some extent in the second half of the epic and, usually even more distinctly, in *PR* and *SA*. *PL* VII and VIII are the points from which the trend back towards the situation in the early pastoral play begins most frequently to develop steadily through several books, whereas the last books of the epic repeatedly relapse toward the practice of the early books. *PL* III, which shows special features, will be discussed at length at the end of this paper, together with the evidence regarding this book to be presented in the following sections.

An interesting feature is the closeness of the links between *PR* and *SA*. Although the former is an epic and the latter a drama, these works, contrary to the theory that "decorum" primarily determines the metrical structure, appear so similar in so many respects that they could hardly be redated separately. Yet since these works mostly continue tendencies characteristic of the second half of *PL*, the impression is strong that they were composed after this part of the poem. These are tentative conclusions which will have to be subjected to further tests.

The initial contrast with *Comus* in *PL* need not surprise one, considering the long interval separating the two works—a period filled with experiences which led to a thorough remolding of Milton's personality. The Milton who wrote *PL* is in many ways an entirely different person from the poet of the masque. It is not surprising to see this change reflected in a renewal of his metrical patterns. Besides, we know too little about the experiments that he may possibly have made in preparation for the main poetical task of his life. The available poetical output from 1634—the date of *Comus*—to the fifties of the century, when Milton is usually supposed to have embarked upon the composition of *PL*, is scanty; nor is it strictly comparable with the verse examined in this paper, since none of it, except a few lines in the prose works, is in blank verse. Nevertheless, certain rhythmical features characteristic of the early books of *PL* do begin to appear in the later rhymed pentameters of Milton—for instance, from about 1645 onwards, a greater number of strong medial pauses. In the rhymed verse written by Milton up to 1645, such pauses are rare. The highest frequency before that date—an exceptional one—is five such pauses in the 34 lines of the second poem "On the University Carrier" (= 14.4 per 100 lines). In the later poems the percentages are often much higher. The first sonnet on "Tetrachordon" and the sonnet "On the late Massacher in Piemont" have five strong medial pauses each (= 35.7 per 100 lines). In the sixteen lines of the version of the Fifth Ode of Horace there are likewise five (31.2 per 100 lines), and the translation of Psalm II, made on August 8, 1653—i.e., probably close to the time when Milton was on the point of beginning his work on *PL*—has 9 in 28 lines (32.1 per 100 lines). Bold medial pauses appear even in the short lines of certain other psalms translated in the same month, e.g., in Psalms III and V. So, evidence is not entirely lacking to suggest certain gradual changes in Milton's rhythm which brought his verse closer to the early patterns of *PL:* the new rhythmical designs do not appear totally unanticipated.[13]

13. It may seem likewise significant that the proportion of rhymed pentameters without any final punctuation becomes especially high in some of the poems of the same period: eight such lines (57.1%) in the sonnets "When I consider how my light is spent" and "Lawrence of vertuous Father vertuous son"; eleven (78.6%) in the sonnet *On the late Massacher;* and twenty (71.4%) in Psalm II. These are figures approached only once in an earlier poem of Milton's, *At a Solemn Musick,* with twelve such pentameters in a total of 25 (48.0%). The second highest percentage in a poem probably written before 1645 is 42.8% in the sonnet *To a Vertuous Young Lady,* the date of which seems to fall within the early forties.

II

TREATMENT OF POLYSYLLABLES

The handling of polysyllables—hardly much less distinctive a feature of Milton's technique than his treatment of pauses—has a somewhat similar history. His rhythmical effects often depend largely on the long words dominating a line, and his predilection for such words appears very clearly in his early poetry. But, as in the case of the pauses, it is some time before he uses them freely in the earlier part of a line. The special effects produced by the polysyllables are at first mainly confined to the second half of his pentameters.

This applies above all to the longest words, those most difficult to handle, but most effective when used skillfully. It is to these that the following analyses will be restricted. For the purposes of the present study, only words of at least four metrical units will count as "polysyllables," and the expression will be understood to refer only to such words. This means that in such a line as *PL* III.373 ("Immutable, Immortal, Infinite") only the first word will be taken into account. Such a word as *spiritual,* though tetrasyllabic in present-day speech, and probably also in Milton's time, is ignored when, as he generally does, he makes it fill only two or three metrical places, as in *PR* I.10 ("Against the Spiritual Foe, and broughtst him thence") or in *PL* XII.518 and 521. *Contagion* is counted in *Comus* 467, where it has the archaic pronunciation, but not in *PL* V.880 and X.544, where it is trisyllabic. *Tartarean* in *PL* II.69 is not counted, because of the elision in the ending. And so forth.

In the following two tables Milton's polysyllables are grouped in three categories: (1) *i*—polysyllabic words commencing in the first or second metrical place; (2) *t*—those placed at the end of a line or ending immediately before the tenth place; and (3) *m*—those in intermediate positions (*i* = initial or near-initial, *t* = terminal or near-terminal, *m* = middle).

TABLE 8

DISTRIBUTION OF POLYSYLLABLES OVER THE VERSE LINE
(Absolute figures)

Comus	6i+9m+38t=53	(66.9 per 1000 lines)
PL I	25i+13m+14t=52	(65.1 " " ")
II	35i+37m+22t=94	(89.1 " " ")
III	25i+29m+20t=74	(99.7 " " ")
IV	29i+17m+11t=57	(56.1 " " ")
V	31i+34m+14t=79	(87.4 " " ")
VI	38i+30m+15t=83	(91.0 " " ")
I-VI	183i+160m+96t=439	(80.9 " " ")
VII	26i+28m+13t=67	(104.7 " " ")
VIII	19i+35m+15t=69	(106.3 " " ")
IX	32i+27m+21t=80	(67.3 " " ")
X	45i+29m+33t=107	(96.9 " " ")
XI	19i+24m+13t=56	(62.4 " " ")
XII	18i+22m+8t=48	(74.5 " " ")
VII-XII	159i+165m+103t=427	(83.3 " " ")
I-XII	342i+325m+199t=866	(82.1 " " ")
PR I	10i+14m+5t=29	(57.8 " " ")
II	9i+15m+8t=32	(65.8 " " ")
III	29i+16m+18t=63	(142.2 " " ")
IV	17i+11m+19t=47	(73.6 " " ")
I-IV	65i+56m+50t=171	(82.6 " " ")
SA	40i+55m+41t=136	(101.6 " " ")

In Table 10, I give the absolute frequencies of polysyllables beginning in the first metrical place, which are indicated by an *a*, and those at the end of lines, designated by the symbol *b*.

The differences in the frequencies per thousand lines for each work considered as a whole display some interesting features, recalling our earlier statistical patterns. *Comus* has the lowest frequency, those for *PL* and *PR* are almost identical, and *SA* reaches the highest point. If we also consider the totals for *PL* I-VI and *PL* VII-XII, we obtain an even clearer

TABLE 9

DISTRIBUTION OF POLYSYLLABLES OVER THE VERSE LINE

(Percentages)

Comus	11.3i+17.0m+71.7t
PL I	48.1i+25.0m+26.9t
II	37.2i+39.4m+23.4t
III	33.8i+39.2m+27.0t
IV	50.8i+29.8m+19.3t
V	39.2i+43.0m+17.7t
VI	45.8i+36.1m+18.1t
I-VI	41.7i+36.4m+21.9t
VII	38.8i+41.8m+19.4t
VIII	27.5i+50.7m+21.7t
IX	40.0i+33.7m+26.2t
X	42.1i+27.1m+30.8t
XI	33.9i+42.9m+23.2t
XII	37.5i+45.8m+16.7t
VII-XII	37.2i+38.6m+24.1t
I-XII	39.5i+37.5m+23.0t
PR I	34.5i+48.3m+17.2t
II	28.1i+46.9m+25.0t
III	46.0i+25.4m+28.6t
IV	36.2i+23.4m+40.4t
I-IV	38.0i+32.7m+29.2t
SA	29.4i+40.4m+30.1t

picture: a rising movement from *Comus* to the end of *PL*, a very slight drop in *PR*, and a further rise in *SA*.

Nevertheless, the differences in the totals for the four works and for the first and the second half of *PL* are not very marked, the greatest difference—that between *SA* and *Comus*—being only 34.7 per thousand lines. There are greater ones between individual books of *PL*—Book VIII exceeding Book IV by as much as 50.2—and especially of *PR*, where Book I, with 57.8 per thousand lines, has the second lowest figure in the entire column, whereas Book III has the highest

TABLE 10

POLYSYLLABLES AT THE BEGINNING AND THE END OF LINES

Comus	1a : 28b	
PL I	8a : 10b	
II	17a : 6b	
III	15a : 10b	
IV	13a : 3b	
V	12a : 5b	
VI	18a : 4b	
I-VI	83a : 38b	
VII	13a : 7b	
VIII	9a : 11b	
IX	14a : 8b	
X	23a : 19b	
XI	5a : 2b	
XII	9a : 5b	
VII-XII	73a : 52b	
I-XII	156a : 90b	
PR I	6a : 4b	
II	1a : 5b	
III	12a : 11b	
IV	7a : 12b	
I-IV	26a : 32b	
SA	14a : 23b	

frequency, 142.2 per thousand lines. Books II and III, V and VI, VII and VIII of *PL*, and Books I and II of *PR* appear closely linked. The break after *PL* VI is again rather marked, and the tendency displayed in Books VII and VIII agrees with the general trend towards an increase in the frequencies observable in the lower part of the column. Much more significant and clear-cut features will become apparent, however, as soon as we examine the distribution of polysyllables over the verse line.

We shall first consider Table 10, giving the frequencies at the beginning and at the end of lines, the positions where the most conspicuous effects are likely to be achieved. Even more drastically than in the case of the pauses, a change takes place between *Comus* and *PL* I, with a strong shift from the end of the line to the beginning. In *Comus* the only initial word of more than three syllables is in line 439, "Antiquity from the old schools of Greece," whereas there are twenty-eight instances of such expressions at the end of lines. In *PL* I the two extremes are almost evenly balanced. Then, from *PL* II to *PL* VI, the beginning decisively predominates; but from *PL* VII to *PL* X there is a gradual, if somewhat wavering, movement in the opposite direction, with actual predominance of the final position in Book VIII. In the last two books we find a relapse, but only a relatively moderate one, especially if we compare it with the situation in Books II, IV, and VI. The first two books of *PR* show sharply contrasting figures, but have few instances of either type. In Book III the ratio is again much as in *PL* X, and in Book IV it comes near to *PL* VIII and is almost the same as in *SA*. The totals for the first and the second half of *PL*, for *PR*, and for *SA* show an increasing use of the final position.

While the figures nowhere resemble those in *Comus*, the tendency from *PL* VII onwards—a turning point with which we are becoming increasingly familiar—though not quite steady, is definitely back towards a situation much more like that in the early poem. It is again as though a period of bold rhythmical innovation in a certain direction were followed by a gradual reaction against it. The last two books of *PL* here, as before, show a temporary weakening of that reaction. The ends of *PR* and *SA* seem to be firmly linked.

Table 9, in which all words of four or more metrical units are included, shows the same tendencies as the figures just discussed. In *Comus* the ratio of such words in the first part of the line—*i*—to those in the final part—*t*—is approximately 1 to 7, whereas in *PL* I it is approximately 5 to 3. In the first half of *PL* the predominance of *i* over *t* is considerable, whereas after Book VI it decreases, being least pronounced in Book X, but again increasing somewhat in the last two books, Book XII coming very close to Book I of *PR*. In *PR* I-IV, *i* loses and *t* gains: the movement started in *PL* VII is continued. It persists in *SA*, where the polysyllables in the first and the last part of the line are almost evenly balanced.

The column for *t*, if considered by itself, is astonishing for the continuity of the pattern it presents. From *Comus* to *PL* V the frequencies decline, with only one slight upward movement in *PL* III; the figures for *PL* V and VI are almost identical. From *PL* VII to *PL* X, the percentages rise steadily; then they decrease in Books XI and XII, the frequency in the last book of the poem being very similar to that in the first book of the next work, *PR*, where a continuous upward climb sets in. The total for *PR* is very close to that for *SA*. Milton's employment of polysyllables towards the end of the verse line—a practice adopted by him at an early date—is much less wavering than that near the beginning of the line, perhaps because in the latter case he is more experimental, trying out his technical moves on less familiar ground.

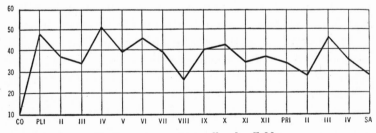

H—*Percentages of* i *in all polysyllables*

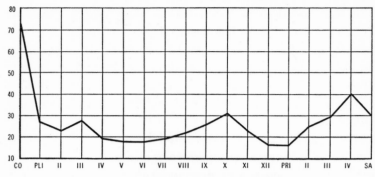

I—*Percentages of* t *in all polysyllables*

The impression created by the above statistical patterns, with regard to both the use of strong pauses and that of polysyllables, is that there is organic development if we assume Milton's works and their parts to have been composed roughly in the order in which they were printed. New vigorous tendencies in the first half of *PL* increasingly lose their vigor in the second half, with Book VII frequently forming the turning point, but a slight reaction often taking place towards the end of the poem. *PR* thereupon develops the trend of the latter half of the earlier epic, repeatedly starting at the point where *PL* leaves off. *SA* then continues the trend of *PR*. The drama again closely resembles the later epic.

Artistically, the problem of pauses and that of polysyllables seem to belong together. In both cases Milton extends his prosodic experiments to the first half of his iambic pentameters as his technique develops. Then, after fully exploring the ground, he moderates his attitude, and a relative, or even complete, balance is achieved.

It is instructive to compare Milton's use of polysyllables with that of Marlowe and Shakespeare. All Marlowe's plays and all Shakespeare's, except only *All's Well That Ends Well* and *Macbeth*, have more polysyllables near the end of the

line than in the middle or near the beginning. In Marlowe
the incidence of terminal and near-terminal polysyllables is
usually about 70 per cent, as in *Comus*. In Shakespeare, up
to about 1594 (assuming Chambers' chronology to be correct), it is, as a rule, fairly close to 60 per cent; from then on
it tends to increase. Then, from *Hamlet* onwards, the incidence suddenly drops to between 40 and 50 per cent, the
only exceptions prior to *Coriolanus* being *Measure for Measure* (54.1 per cent), *All's Well That Ends Well* (25.6 per
cent) and *Macbeth* (35.5 per cent). The parts of *Pericles*
usually ascribed to Shakespeare (53.7 per cent), *Coriolanus*
(50.6 per cent), *Cymbeline* (53.3 per cent), and *The
Tempest* (52.6 per cent) again have somewhat higher
figures. The percentages for plays which on the basis of
other evidence must be supposed to belong to identical
periods are often remarkably alike, e.g., those for 2 *Henry
VI* (15.7i+19.1m+65.2t), 3 *Henry VI* (16.5i+20.9m+62.6t),
Titus Andronicus (15.2i+25.6m+59.2t), and *Richard III*
(17.4i+22.6m+60.0t); for *The Merchant of Venice* (10.1i+
17.4m+72.5t), *Julius Caesar* (13.7i+14.4m+71.8t), and
Much Ado About Nothing (7.5i+17.5m+75.0t); for *Timon
of Athens* (25.9i+30.6m+43.5t) and *King Lear* (22.7i+
30.9m+46.4t); for *Coriolanus* (18.4i+31.0m+50.6t), *Cymbeline* (16.2i+30.5m+53.3t) and *The Tempest* (19.2i+
28.1m+52.6t). The development is like Milton's in that
the predominance of terminal and near-terminal polysyllables diminishes as Shakespeare reaches complete maturity.
The drift towards the end of the line in the latest plays also
constitutes a parallel, albeit a faint one.

As the figures presented above—to which others, from
Dekker, Greene, Chapman, and Ben Jonson might be added
—suggest, the use of polysyllables in *Comus* seems to be
typically Elizabethan, conforming to a practice apparently
started by Marlowe, whereas in Milton's later works it is *sui
generis*. Only in *All's Well That Ends Well* and in *Macbeth*

have I come across figures at all resembling those of Milton's mature work.[14]

III

FEMININE ENDINGS

In his article "The Date of Samson Agonistes" Professor W. R. Parker dismisses the problem of the feminine endings in Milton's blank verse as of little value for the study of chronological problems.[15] Actually, a close examination of them would appear to be of the greatest interest, both on its own account and for determining the relative chronology of Milton's works. Perhaps even more distinctly than the aspects of his versification already examined, the feminine endings show definite changes of technique which deserve to be carefully scrutinized.

14. As for the distribution of strong pauses in *Comus*, it shows a marked resemblance to that in Shakespeare's latest plays. Shakespeare's early plays, like those of Marlowe, show a decided preference for pauses in the first half of the line, mainly after the fourth syllable—a practice apparently adopted from Surrey, Gascoigne, Sackville and Norton, and other early writers of blank verse. There is relatively little experimentation with pauses in this verse, which, regardless of the type of drama, tends to adhere rather closely to a stereotyped scheme. Strong pauses in extreme positions are very rare. As Shakespeare proceeds, the balance, again irrespective of the type of play, gradually shifts towards the second half of the line, until in *Coriolanus* we find proportions closely resembling those in *Comus*. The use of extreme pauses increases, but mainly near the end of the pentameter line. This development in Shakespeare, so different from that in Milton, may perhaps be partly explained by the increasing looseness in the structure of his blank verse, the rhythm of which in the late plays would not always be easily recognizable if the verse line were not permitted to get into its stride before the introduction of any heavy pauses. It is characteristic that in these plays strong pauses in the last third of the line are about nine times as frequent as in the first third, and the frequency of strong pauses after the sixth syllable is about twice that of such pauses after the fourth syllable. Milton's blank verse, with its firmer texture, seems to have required no such precautions. The above observations are based on a detailed study of some aspects of Shakespeare's prosody on which I am engaged.

15. Parker, 155.

In the following pages I shall examine Milton's feminine endings; but I shall exclude from consideration those forms which Milton predominantly, or in some cases always, uses as monosyllables, and which are clearly capable of mono-syllabic or near-monosyllabic pronunciation: *power, hour, flower, shower, tower, bower, lour, scour, (over)powered, (em)powered, (de)vour, heaven, given, (for)given, seven, seventh, risen, fallen, driven, even.*

Counted with this reservation, the absolute totals of feminine endings and (in parenthesis) their frequencies per thousand lines are as follows:

Comus: 81 (102.3).
PL: (a) I—10 (12.5); II—9 (8.5); III—8 (10.7); IV—4 (3.9); V—7 (7.7); VI—3 (3.2). Total for *PL* I-VI: 41 (7.6).

   (b) VII—4 (6.2); VIII—12 (18.5); IX—20 (16.8); X—53 (48.0); XI—4 (4.4); XII—13 (20.2). Total for *PL* VII-XII: 106 (20.6).

Total for *PL* I-XII: 147 (13.0).
PR: I—20 (39.8); II—8 (16.4); III—32 (72.2); IV—31 (48.5). Total 91 (43.7).
SA: 242 (180.8).

As we see, *SA* is an easy first as regards the frequency of feminine endings, followed at some distance by *Comus*. *PR* lags far behind *Comus*, and *PL* far behind *PR*. There is doubtless much justification for Professor Parker's view that the special attitude in *SA* and *Comus* is attributable to the fact that both are dramatic pieces.[16] It deserves to be noted, however, that *SA* avails itself of this dramatic convention to an exceptionally great extent—almost twice as frequently as the early masque. And what is still more notable is the development in *PL* and *PR*. Throughout *PL* I-VI the frequencies are remarkably low, reaching a minimum in Book

16. *Ibid.*

VI, but then—at the familiar turning point, Book VII, up to another point that has repeatedly been found to mark a provisional climax for developments begun in Book VII, viz., Book X—the figures increase, at first slowly, then in Book X, at a sudden leap. Books XI and XII again have lower figures, Book XI dropping to the third-lowest level in the poem. Then, in *PR*, we have a pronounced though not continuous increase, Book III reaching a figure only about one-third lower than that for *Comus*. *SA* thereupon represents a culmination far exceeding even *Comus*. It is the old pattern with which we are thoroughly familiar by now, save that in the present case *SA* outdistances the maximum figure in *PR* to an extent not encountered before— most probably because a tendency progressively noticeable in Milton's nondramatic poems is here reinforced by a convention peculiar to the dramatic genre.[17]

17. Although the speeches in *PL* and *PR* have, on the whole, a higher proportion of feminine endings than the narrative parts, numerous passages occur in *PL* in which the opposite is the case. Such passages are especially frequent in the second half of *PL*, where the total percentage for the speeches only very slightly exceeds that for the narrative. The narrative in *PL* VII-XII has a higher incidence of feminine endings than the speeches in *PL* I-VI. The tendency to use more and more such endings, however, is more pronounced in the speeches than in the narrative. This becomes especially clear in *PR*. The figures are as follows:

	Speeches	Narrative
PL I-VI:	27 (14.0 per 1000 lines)	14 (4.6 per 1000 lines)
VII-XII:	56 (21.5 ” ” ”)	48 (18.7 ” ” ”)
PR I-IV:	86 (55.0 ” ” ”)	5 (9.9 ” ” ”)

The evidence for *PL* VII-XII suggests that there the growing predilection for double endings can have little if anything to do with dramatic decorum. In *PR* the line between the epic and the dramatic parts may indeed have been drawn more consciously. However, there is so little narrative that it is difficult to draw any very definite conclusions. The speeches in *PR*, with their greatly increased number of double endings, confirm the impression of a growing, probably spontaneous, change in rhythmical taste. The high figure in *SA*—so much higher than any earlier ones—seems natural if viewed as a result of this trend, considerably intensified by the dramatic tradition.

Sprott, p. 58, suggests the decline in epic dignity in parts of the second half of *PL* as the reason for Milton's increasing use of feminine endings. One wonders, however, why this criterion of dignity was not applied in

Even more interesting facts emerge as we examine the phonetic nature of the feminine endings—as our quantitative analysis is supplemented by a qualitative one.

For convenience' sake we shall start not with *Comus* but with *PL*, where certain striking differences will be found as the poem progresses. We shall thereafter examine *PR* and *SA*, and then finally compare our results with the evidence found in *Comus*. The material from *PL* I-VI, which is of special interest and not very extensive, must be adduced in full. The expressions used for feminine endings, quoted in the order of their occurrence, are as follows:

Book I: *aspiring* (38), *merit* (98), *preferring* (102), *being* (154), *miserable* (157), *evil* (165), *Thunder* (174), *rather* (606), *grav'n* (716), *Ceremony* (753).

Book II: *exposes* (27), *Spirit* (44), *being* (98, 147), *inevitable* (197), *preferring* (255), *engraven* (302), *being* (440), *viewing* (764).

Book III: *disobeying* (203), *merit* (290), *enjoying* (306), *being* (374), *Friers* (474), *Luminarie* (576), *tiar* (626), *hither* (698).

Book IV: *higher* (50), *dishonorable* (314), *forbidd'n* (515), *hither* (908).

Book V: *offended* (135), *being* (455), *tending* (476), *being* (487), *Spirit* (497), *being* (822, 855).

Book VI: *innumerable* (82), *Highest* (114), *unconquerable* (118).

A peculiarity that strikes one in going through this list is the relatively small number of different forms used—twenty-eight in a total of forty-one instances of feminine endings. One word, *being*, occurs eight times; *merit, spirit, preferring*, and *hither* appear twice each; and *grav'n* and *engraven*

PR. Had Milton's experimentation with double endings in *PL* VII-XII satisfied him that his original stylistic restrictions were excessive and that such endings were fully capable of expressing dignity while adding variety to the style? Compare Spenser's introduction of feminine rhymes into the second part of the *Faerie Queene.*

also are practically identical from our point of view. Milton seems to have had special preferences with regard to the forms he employed for feminine endings. This suspicion is strengthened if one studies the phonetic composition of the endings in our list, for then one discovers an almost total absence of unvoiced consonants. The only exceptions are five cases in which such consonants occur after the unstressed vowel of the final syllable, i.e., in the position in which they are least obtrusive: *merit* (I.98, III.290), *spirit* (II.44, V.497), *Highest* (VI.114). The only consonantal groups appearing between the stressed and the unstressed vowels of the verse endings are two unusually light ones: *-nd-* and *-bl-*, and even these occur in only eight instances: *miserable* (I.157), *inevitable* (II.197), *dishonorable* (IV.314), *innumerable* (VI.82), *unconquerable* (VI.118), *Thunder* (I.174), *offended* (V.135), *tending* (V.476). Otherwise, there are in this position only single voiced consonants or no consonants at all.

As would almost follow from this description, and as we actually find on further scrutiny, a considerable number of these endings belong to categories that Milton often tends, by way of elision or contraction, fictive or real, to treat as monosyllables when they occur within the line. Many of them, in terms of Milton's prosody as expounded by Robert Bridges, might be counted as monosyllables as they stand, whereas others belong to types frequently elided when followed by a vowel.

The following endings could be regarded as monosyllabic or equivalent to monosyllables as we have them in the text: (1) *higher*—cf. "The greedy flame runs hier and hier" (Psalm LXXXIII.55); (2) *tiar;* (3) *Friers;* (4) *Highest*—cf. *PL* II. 630, VI.205; (5) *being* (8 instances)—cf. *PL* II.585, IV.483; (6) *viewing*—cf. *doing PL* II.162, *ruin PL* I.91; (7) *(en)joying* —cf. *flying PL* II.942, *dying PL* X.974; (8) *(disob)eying*—cf. *saying PL* VI.189; (9) *spirit* (2 instances)—mostly used as at least theoretically monosyllabic throughout the poem; (10) *grav'n, (en)graven*—cf. *chos'n PL* I.318.

So, altogether nineteen of the forty-one feminine endings in Books I-VI—46.4 per cent—belong to types often, or in some cases even predominantly, treated by Milton as monosyllabic at least in theory. This applies to the above types regardless of whether they occur before a consonant or a vowel.

As for the remaining twenty-two instances, only eight of them are such that they apparently could not in any circumstances be subjected to elision or contraction: *aspiring, merit* (2 instances), *preferring* (2 instances), *exposes, offended, tending.* And even in these cases, as in all the rest, we find a notable absence of heavy endings. The heaviest final syllable in our list is *-est* in *Highest,* and this occurs in a case which lends itself to monosyllabic interpretation.

It seems permissible to infer that, on the few occasions when Milton uses feminine endings in *PL* I-VI, he tries to keep them as light as possible—so much so as with regard to nearly half of them almost to make it seem doubtful, considering his special prosody, whether he intended them to be interpreted as feminine endings at all.[18]

The situation changes as we get to Book VII. The frequency of feminine endings increases only slightly, but their

18. See also Walter Thomas, "Milton's Heroic Line," *MLR,* III (1907), 19; J. C. Smith, "Feminine Endings in Milton's Blank Verse," *TLS,* Dec. 5, 1936, p. 1016; and E. P. Morton, p. 95. All these critics note the lightness of Milton's feminine endings and point out their growing frequency in his later work. Thomas also notices Milton's tendency to use as feminine endings words which he elsewhere contracts. Sprott develops this idea at greater length, arriving at conclusions (ch. VI) rather similar to those advanced in the present paper. A bold but not impossible suggestion of his is the idea that Milton may sometimes have intended elision between the ending of one line and the beginning of the next. He gives no figures for such instances, however. According to my own count, four endings in *PL* I-VI, five in *PL* VII-XII, five in *PR,* and twenty-two in *SA* might be affected if this possibility were assumed.

quality is different. The categories of Books I to VI continue to appear, but there are such forms as *Tabernacle* (248) and *rèceptacle* (307) which contain unvoiced consonants—in this case perhaps the harshest type of them, unvoiced plosives—after the stressed vowel. Book VIII has two such forms: *delicacies* (526) and *expressing* (544), as well as two examples with unvoiced consonants after an unstressed vowel: *supposest* (86) and *satietie* (216). In Book IX we find *asperses* (296), *presented* (974), *overtrusting* (1183); and *societie* (249). Book X has *alienated* (378), *expecting* (439, 504), *election* (764), *torment me* (781), *revolution* (814), *represented* (849), *meeting* (879), *relented* (940), *seeking* (943), *light'n* (960), *expected* (1048); and *enterprisest* (270), *perish* (785), *exercise not* (927), *cherish* (1068). There are no examples of either category in Book XI, but Book XII has *Tabernacle* (247), *representing* (255), *appropriating* (518); and *obedience* (408), *merits* (409).

Save for Book XI—already found to be exceptional for the second half of the poem as regards its low total frequency of feminine endings—the new taste for unvoiced consonants and for harsher consonantal combinations persists throughout. It is also noteworthy that *sh*—a sound which in general Milton avoids—begins to appear: *election, revolution, perish, cherish*. A new feature not found at all in any previous part of *PL* is the use of separate words for the final unstressed syllable in Book X: *torment me* (781), *from thee* (871), *assign'd us* (926), *exercise not* (927). This means weighting that syllable to an extent unprecedented in the poem. The dactylic endings *satietie, societie* are also novel as far as *PL* is concerned; both, however, are theoretically convertible into trochees, as so many of the trochaic endings of Books I to VI seem in theory to be convertible into long monosyllabic beats.[19]

19. See Thomas, 18.

In *PR* we encounter a situation much like that in *PL* VII-XII, as the following lists show:

A. Unvoiced consonants after the last stressed vowel:
Book I: *written* (347), *representing* (418), *afflict him* (425), *permit me* (483).
Book II: *content me* (256).
Book III: *àttributed* (69), *exemption* (115), *violated* (160), *expecting* (192), *inquisition* (200), *destruction* (202), *united* (229), *unadventrous* (243), *Successour* (373).
Book IV: *suspicious* (96), *utter* (172), *condition* (173), *written* (175), *worship* (176), *Paradoxes* (234), *possessing* (302), *personating* (341), *teaching* (357), *preventing* (492), *accepting* (493), *written* (560), *expressing* (601).
B. Unvoiced consonants after the last unstressed vowel:
Book I: *highest* (139).
Book II: *need not* (249).
Book III: *highest* (30), *merit* (196), *unadventrous* (243).
Book IV: *suspicious* (96), *worship* (176), *brings not* (323), *discern not* (390).
C. Unvoiced consonants after the first unstressed vowel in dactylic ending:
Book I: *Society* (302).

Nearly everything that has been said concerning the feminine endings of *PL* VII-XII might be repeated here. It may be worth noting that the same word as in *PL* X, *Society,* is used in *PR* I as a dactylic "feminine" ending. Another dactylic ending, *Deliverers,* occurs in *PR* III.82. It is also theoretically, and even in actual pronunciation, reducible to a trochaic ending, but by a different method: the suppression of a vowel rather than the diphthongization of contiguous vowels. Endings with a separate word constituting the final unstressed syllable have become more frequent than in *PL:* *afflict him* (I.425), *permit me* (I.483), *reveal'd him* (II.50), *need not* (II.249), *content me* (II.256), *reinstall thee* (III. 372), *leave them* (III.440), *brings not* (IV.323), *discern not* (IV.390), *fear them* (IV.454), *found thee* (IV.532).

All the features noted from the second half of *PL* to *PR* continue throughout *SA*. The evidence—eighty-six instances of unvoiced consonants after the stressed vowel of the ending (35.5 per cent of the total number of feminine endings), thirty-six of such consonants after the unstressed vowel (14.5 per cent)—is too voluminous to be quoted in full. The stressed part of the endings often has such consonantal groups as -st- (*trusting* [1178], *jester* [1338], *resistless* [1405], *requested* [1630], *unjustly* [889]), -ct- (*afflicts me* [195], *exact not* [788], *afflict thee* [1252], *inflicted* [485]; cf. also -ksh-: *affection* [739], *subjection* [1405]), -ft- (*bereft me* [48], *Caphtor* [1713], *safety* [780]), -nt- (*countrey* [1208], *consented* [846], *circumvent me* [1115]), -lt- (*consulted* [1546], *frailty* [783]), -kn- (*weakness* [235, 773]), -tn- (*witness* [239]), -tcr- (*outcry* [1517]), and other "harsh" combinations, not to mention cases of single plosives and sibilants. There are fifty-nine instances (22.6 per cent of the total) of composite endings, often with a heavy word forming the final syllable, e.g., *not* (782, 788, 1368, 1553), *thee* (874, 921, 1102, 1117, 1123, 1126, 1160, 1183, 1237, 1243, 1252, 1552), or even *men* in *àll men* (938). The dactylic endings demand special notice: *deliverance* (603), *importuning* (797), *authority* (868), *ridiculous* (1361), *heaviest* (445). Except for *heaviest*, which permits at least fictive diphthongization of the vowels involved (like *satiety* and *society* in *PL* and *PR*), all these forms require the suppression of a vowel between two consonants if they are—in theory or reality—to be reduced to the trochaic norm, as seemed possible with regard to all previously noted instances of dactylic endings. Such a procedure seems quite conceivable in respect to *deliverance, importuning,* and *ridiculous,* but there appear to be greater difficulties in the case of *authority.* Milton is employing less and less contractible forms for his dactylic endings; in this respect, too, his technique becomes bolder and freer.

So, our examination of Milton's feminine endings yields the familiar conclusion that *SA* seems to stand at the end of a development beginning in *PL VII*. In the tragedy tendencies clearly perceptible in the latter half of *PL* as well as throughout *PR* would appear to reach their final and highest point—expansive tendencies making for greater freedom of technique than the first half of *PL* seemed to permit.

On the basis of our previous analyses we should almost expect this ultimate point to get fairly near to the practice of *Comus*. This is precisely what we find. *Comus* shares most of the features that begin to appear, or to become more frequent, from *PL* VII onwards: (1) unvoiced consonants after the stressed vowel of the endings (*listed* [49], *Circe* [50], *count'nance* [68], *Wildernesses* [209], *attention* [258], *Echo* [275], etc.—altogether 33 cases = 46.7 per cent); or (2) after the unstressed vowel (*Servants* [10], *vengeance* [218], *farthest* [227], *attention* [258], etc.—21 cases = 25.9 per cent); (3) the use of separate words for the final syllable, often heavy ones—even heavier in some cases than any in *SA* (*thìs soyl* [633], *stàkes else* [491]—altogether 12 cases = 14.8 per cent); (4) dactylic endings (*likeliest* [192], *diamonds* [732], *riotous* [763]). As regards this last category, however, it is remarkable that the instances cited—the only ones in the 1645 edition—are all contractible by diphthongizing the contiguous vowels. It is not until the 1673 edition that we find two additional examples that cannot be contracted by this method. Line 474—in the first edition "And link'd it self by carnal sensualty"—becomes "And link't it self by carnal sensuality"; and line 547 ("To meditate my rural minstrelsie") appears as "To meditate upon my rural minstrelsie." *Sensuality* belongs to a type very similar to *authority* in *SA;* both resemble *minstrelsie* in the difficulty of thinking of them as even theoretically contractible.[20] These changes were almost certainly made in Milton's latest period, and they suggest that such an ending as *authority* prob-ably also belongs to that period, especially since no similar instances occur in the two epics.

Rejecting with Professor W. R. Parker the notion that the similarities in the use of feminine endings in *Comus* and *SA* could be utilized to infer any chronological proximity between them,[21] I tentatively suggest a different theory. As in the cases of strong medial pauses and polysyllables, Milton, by the time he began to write *PL*—at least in its final form—had arrived at a position very far removed from that which he held in *Comus*. This position he maintained throughout the first half of the poem, which (according to our evidence) seems to have been composed more or less continuously. But when he began to compose Book VII— perhaps after an interval possibly caused by the troubles connected with the Restoration, as Professor J. H. Hanford suggests[22]—his technique became freer. He gradually took in more and more of the devices which he had already ex-

20. *Sensuality* and *authority* would, however, come under those cases which Bridges (*Milton's Prosody*, p. 30) lists as exceptional types of elision occurring mainly in *PR* and *SA*. The only words in *PL* in which unstressed *i* before *t* seems to undergo elision are *capital* and *Capitoline;* the first half of the poem has only one instance (*capital* in II.924), whereas there are three in the second half (*Capitoline* IX.508; *capital* XI.343, XII.383). *PR* III.400 has *politic;* *SA* has *magnanimity* (1470), *calamitous* (1480). The fact that Milton elides this phonetic combination in mid-verse would seem to support the conception of the last two syllables of *authority* and *sensuality* as theoretically contractible extrametrical parts of pentameters, rather than as hexameter elements.

The case of *minstrelsie*, for which no elided equivalents within the line are found, is for this reason more doubtful: it may not have been intended to be a dactylic "feminine" ending. It is in any case interesting to observe the close parallelism with which the trend for greater metrical freedom appears both in the phonetic types chosen for elision and in those used as dactylic endings.

21. Parker, 155.

22. J. H. Hanford, *John Milton, Englishman* (New York, 1949), p. 172

ploited in *Comus,* and eventually added some not yet used there, such as the *authority-sensuality* type of ending, which seems definitely late. In *SA,* partly because it is a drama and makes use of the traditional dramatic licenses, and partly because it is a final manifestation of tendencies which had become apparent much earlier, in Milton's epic work, all these features appear in a pronounced form—in some respects more pronounced even than in *Comus.*

IV

RHYTHMICAL TYPE: "COMPLEAT STEEL—DIVINE PROPERTY"

Milton does not always in his later work tend to revert to his early methods. Certain practices disappear or become rare. Such a case is that of the rhythmical type appearing in the phrases "divine property" (*Comus* 469) and "compleat steel" (*ibid.* 421), viz., an adjective or participle usually accented on the last syllable, followed by a noun beginning with a stressed syllable, with the adjective so placed that its stressed syllable occupies a normally unstressed metrical position. This feature is not uncommon in Shakespeare, e.g., in *Hamlet:* "upon my secure hour" (I.v.61), "obscure funeral" (IV.v.213), "complete steel" (I.iv.52)—this last the very expression that Milton uses in *Comus,* perhaps copying Shakespeare.[23] Milton's early poetry has some sixteen instances of this type: "supreme Throne" (*On Time* 17), "unshowr'd Grasse" (*Nat. Ode* 215), "serene Ayr" (*Comus* 4), "enthron'd gods" (*ibid.* 11), "perplex't paths" (*ibid.* 37), "Supreme good" (*ibid.* 217), "extreme shift" (*ibid.* 274), "compleat steel" (*ibid.* 421), "unblench't majesty" (*ibid.* 430), "unlaid ghost" (*ibid.* 434), "congeal'd stone" (*ibid.* 449), "unchaste

23. See Bridges, pp. 67-77. Bridges' criticisms of Alexander Schmidt's analysis of this phenomenon (as found in Shakespeare) seem to go too far but cannot be discussed here.

looks" (*ibid.* 464), "divine property" (*ibid.* 469), "unjust force" (*ibid.* 590), "sublime notion" (*ibid.* 785), "unsought diamonds" (*ibid.* 732).

No attempt will be made to decide how far Milton intended the stress in the adjective or participle to undergo recession, as Robert Bridges claims it does, although it seems doubtful whether such a throwback was possible, for instance, in "perplex't paths." There is, however, some probability in Bridges' suggestion that Milton afterwards purposely excluded this type of phrase "for fear of introducing uncertainty into his rhythms, but that the necessity of avoiding it altogether was not at first realized, or that his old habit was not quite conquered."[24] In any case, Books I to IV of *PL* still have a number of instances: "unblest feet" (I.238), "obscene dread" (I.406), "supreme King" (I.735), "obscure wing" (II.132), "Supream Foe" (II.210), "unknown Regions" (II.443), "unknown dangers" (II.444), "confus'd march" (II.615), "oblique way" (III.564), "unpierc't shade" (IV.245). After Book IV the only words that could possibly be regarded as being used in a comparable manner are *upright* ("upright beams" VI.82) and *adverse* ("adverse Legions" VI.206, "adverse blast" X.701). But these are expressions in which a stress-shift in a similar position is still the rule in present-day English. It is probable that this was the case also in Milton's time, so they were hardly likely to cause the rhythmical uncertainty which he may have feared.

It is noteworthy that this rhythmically dubious type seems to be entirely avoided in *PR* as well as in *SA*. That this avoidance is deliberate seems clear from the way in which Milton treats the same or similar phrases when he needs them after *PL* IV, and sometimes even earlier. He takes care to place them so as to make the word stress clearly coincide with the metrical stress, usually by inverting the order of noun and

24. Bridges, p. 73.

adjective (or participle). Compare, e.g., "supreme Throne" (*On Time* 17) with "Throne supream" (*PL* V.667, XI.82); "divine property" (*Comus* 469) with "looks Divine" (*PL* IV.291), "voice Divine" (*PL* VIII.436), "wrath divine" (*SA* 1683); "enthron'd gods" (*Comus* 11) with "God enthron'd" (*PL* V.536). For similar changes of position of *serene* see *PL* VII.509; of *complete*, *PR* IV.283; of *unblest*, *PL* X.988; of *obscure*, *PL* IV.840, X.366, *PR* III.94, *SA* 572. Or if Milton, as he not infrequently does, wants to keep the adjective before the noun, he finds a noun beginning with an unstressed syllable: "supream decree" (*PL* III.659), "divine impulsion" (*SA* 422), "divine disposal" (*SA* 210), "extream contempt" (*SA* 1342), "unjust tribunals" (*SA* 695).[25]

V

SYLLABIZED -ED ENDINGS

A further method of avoiding the rhythmical type discussed in the previous section, if the first part of the phrase is a past participle or participial adjective, is by syllabizing the mute *e* of the ending, e.g., in *unarmed*. Instead of writing "The unarm'd Youth" in *PL* IV. 552, Milton spells "Th' unarmed Youth," thus making *-ed* a separate syllable. All uncertainty concerning the rhythm is thus precluded. Moreover, the increased smoothness of the effect is obvious; there is no longer any suggestion of a clash of stressed syllables. Greater rhythmical smoothness by syllabization of the mute *e* is also attained when the participle in its unlengthened form is monosyllabic. In this case what is avoided is usually a "spondaic" rhythm. See, for instance, "Or fill the fixed mind with all your toyes" (*Il Penseroso* 4) and compare this with

25. Bridges, p. 72, points out that, in *PL*, *divine Semblance* (IX.606) and *supreme Kingdom* (VI.814) are divided between two lines: another of Milton's methods of preventing rhythmical ambiguity.

"Though chang'd in outward lustre; that fixt mind" (*PL* I.97).

This device, perhaps partly because of the rhythmical fluidity, the "mellifluousness" which it enhances, is common in Elizabethan verse, where, however, it already has an archaic flavor. Milton uses it copiously in his early verse and has much of it in the first half of *PL*, but thereafter—possibly as a result of a growing antiarchaic trend or because of his tendency towards vigorous concentration—employs it less and less. The evidence is of such unusual interest for our chronological purposes that it will have to be cited *in extenso*.

A complete list, from which the expressions *blessed, beloved, learned, cursed, crooked*, and *aged* are excluded because they were and commonly (or at least frequently) still are pronounced with a syllabic *e*, is as follows:

I. EARLY PERIOD

Psalm CXIV: froth-becurled head (8). *Psalm CXXXVI:* Amazed Heav'n (13), Golden-tressed Sun (29), horned Moon (32). *Nativity Ode:* hooked Chariot (56), armed throng (58), charmed wave (68), stringed noise (97), helmed Cherubim (112), usurped sway (170), arched roof (175), breathed spell (179), mooned *Ashtaroth* (200), sable-stoled Sorcerers (220), damned crew (228), youngest teemed Star (240). *On The Death of a Fair Infant:* ycie-pearled carr (15), dearly-loved mate (24), low delved tombe (32), white-robed Truth (54), golden-winged hoast (57), præfixed seat (59), deserved smart (69). *Vacation Exercise:* piled Thunder (42). *On Shakespeare:* piled Stones (2). *On a Solemn Music:* undisturbed Song (6). *Upon the Circumcision:* winged Warriours (1). *L'Allegro:* loathed Melancholy (1), Ivy-crowned *Bacchus* (16), Wreathed Smiles (28), unreproved pleasures (40), lincked sweetnes (140). *Il Penseroso:* fixed mind (4), retired Leasure (49), fiery-wheeled throne (53), removed place (78), arched walks (133), heaved stroke (136), embowed Roof (157). *Arcades:* renowned flood (29), grosse unpurged ear (73). *Comus* (blank verse): unadorned boosom of the Deep (24), mis-used Wine (47), charmed Cup (51), retired Solitude (376), unowned sister (407), abhorred rites (535), obscured haunts (536), unarmed weakness (582), uncontrouled worth (793), enraged stepdam (830), pearled wrists (834); (lyrical verse) rushy-fringed bank (890), charmed band (904), insnared chastity (909), brimmed waves (924), singed air (928), crisped shades (983); (cancelled passage) removed climes. *Lycidas:* abhorred shears (75), beaked Promontory (94).

II. Middle Period

Psalm LXXX (1648): Thy loved Josephs seed (4). *Psalm LXXXIII* (1648): their armed hands (31). *To Cromwell* (1652): crowned Fortune (5). *5th Ode of Horace* (?): changed Gods (6).

III. Late Period

A. *Sonnet "On His Deceased Wife"* (1658): my late espoused Saint (1)

B. *Paradise Lost:*

(1) *Book I:* many Throned Powers (128), fixed Anchor (206), wished Morn (208), singed bottom (236), inflamed Sea (300), linked Thunderbolts (328), Grazed Ox (486), fixed thought (560), armed Files (567), singed top (614), grasped arm's (667), arched roof (726), winged Haralds (752), squared Regiment (758), smoothed Plank (772). *Book II:* abhorred deep (87), Armed watch (130), ranged powers (522), obdured brest (568), Abhorred Styx (577), winged course (944). *Book III:* unapproached light (4), lapsed powers (176), incensed Deitie (187), winged messengers (229), fixed seat (669—twice in same line). *Book IV:* crisped Brooks (237), fringed Bank (262), unadorned

golden tresses (305), unarmed Youth (552), winged Warriour (576), Espoused Eve (710), mooned hornes (978).
Book V: winged Saint (247), winged Hierarch (468), Th'
incensed Father, and th' incensed Son (844). *Book VI:*
armed Saints (47), armed Peers (127), armed hand (231),
deformed rout (387), orbed Shield (543), deserved right
(709), Unfained Halleluiahs (744), helmed heads (840).
Cf. also: "light-armed scoure" (VI.529).

(2) *Book VII:* winged Spirits (199), Arched neck (438).
Book VIII: droused sense (289). *Book IX:* no examples.
Book X: forked tongue (518, 519). *Book XI:* winged Steeds
(702), beaked prow (742), horned floud (827). *Book XII:*
no examples.

C. *Paradise Regained:*
Book I: no examples. *Book II:* no examples. *Book III:*
light armed Troops (311). *Book IV:* abhorred pact (191).

D. *Samson Agonistes:*
(Nonlyrical verse) armed powers (1190), armed guards
(1617), arched roof (1634). (Lyrical verse) winged expedi-
tion (1283), perched roosts (1693).

As so often before, we see here a change from *PL* VII
onwards. In the second half of *PL* the use of syllabized -*ed*
endings is reduced to a minimum. This attitude persists in
PR and *SA*.

There are further differences. While a good many trisyllabic, and even tetrasyllabic, expressions of our type occur
in the early poems (*becurlèd, Amazèd, usurpèd, deservèd,
undisturbèd,* etc.—23 cases) as well as in *PL* I-VI (*inflamèd,
abhorrèd, obdurèd, unapproachèd,* etc.—14 cases), the only
later example is *abhorrèd* in *PR*. An interesting case is
espousèd. Outside of *PL* IV it appears only in a sonnet
usually assumed to have been written in 1658, i.e., shortly
before the Restoration, and, if Professor J. H. Hanford is

correct, about the time when *PL* IV may have been composed.[26]

Furthermore, if we compare our lists for the unquestionably early poems with those for *PL*, *PR*, and *SA*, we find that the first half of *PL* has a surprising number of expressions that occur also in the early work. In the second half of *PL*, in *PR*, and in *SA*, on the other hand, this happens very seldom, and the expressions repeated from the early poems nearly always appear also in *PL* I-VI (*armèd, wingèd, abhorrèd, archèd*). The only independent links with the early poems found in our list after *PL* VI are in the description of the Deluge in *PL* XI: *beakèd* in line 746, with which compare *Lycidas*, line 94, and *hornèd* in line 827, with which compare Psalm CXXXVI.32.

Finally, *PL* VII-XII, the whole of *PR*, and *SA* are conspicuous for their scarcity of expressions of our type that do not appear somewhere else (not to use the term "earlier") in Milton's verse—altogether three cases: *drousèd* in *PL* VIII, *forkèd* in *PL* X, and *perchèd* in *SA*. In *PL* I-VI, on the other hand, there are sixteen such forms: *wishèd, inflamèd, Thronèd, grazèd, graspèd, squarèd, smoothèd* in Book I; *rangèd, obdurèd* in Book II; *unapproachèd, lapsèd, incensèd* in Book III; *deformèd, orbèd, light-armèd, unfainèd* in Book VI. It is as though this type of word, still very much alive in *PL* I-VI, had subsequently lost its vitality, surviving mainly in somewhat commonplace echoes from Milton's own recent work.

A close inspection of the verbal parallels between the early work and *PL* I-VI may provide some clues as to what is likely to have happened. The parallels are as follows:

26. See Hanford, p. 173, where the similarity of mood between this sonnet and *PL* IV is pointed out. Professor Parker would like to re-date this sonnet, making it refer to Milton's first wife, Mary Powell, but it seems difficult to accept this theory. See Woodhouse, 172n, and F. Pyle, *RES*, N.S., II (1951), 152-154.

Book I: fixèd (thought, anchor)—fixèd mind
(*Il Penseroso*)
singèd (bottom, top)—singèd air (*Comus*)
linkèd (Thunderbolts)—linckèd sweetness
(*L'Allegro*)
wingèd (Haralds)—wingèd Warriours
(*Circumcision*)
archèd (roof)—*Nat. Ode,* archèd walks
(*Il Penseroso*)
armèd (Files)—armèd throng (*Nat. Ode*)

Book II: abhorrèd (deep, Styx)—abhorrèd rites to
Hecate (*Comus*); the blind fury with th'
abhorrèd shears (*Lycidas*)
armèd (watch)—see under Book I
wingèd (course)—see under Book I

Book III: wingèd (messengers)—see under Book I
fixèd (seat)—see under Book I

Book IV: crispèd (Brooks)—crispèd shades and bowres
(*Comus*)
fringèd (Bank)—rushy-fringèd bank (*Comus*)
unadornèd (golden Tresses)—unadornèd
boosom of the Deep (*Comus*)
unarmèd (Youth)—unarmèd weakness of one
Virgin (*Comus*)
wingèd (Warriours)—see under Book I
moonèd (horns—of phalanx)—moonèd Ashtaroth
(*Nat. Ode*)

Book V: wingèd (Saint, Hierach)—see under Book I

Book VI: helmèd (head—of routed angels)—helmèd
Cherubim (*Nat. Ode*)
deservèd (right)—deservèd smart *Death of a
Fair Infant*
armèd (Peers, Saints, hand)—see under Book I.
Note "armèd hands" in Psalm LXXXII (translated in 1648).

In a number of these parallels we find actual identity of
expression even in the nouns, or otherwise close similarity

of wording or context: "fixèd thought" (*PL* I)—"fixèd mind" (*Il Penseroso*); "archèd roof"—(identical in *PL* I and *Nat. Ode*); "abhorrèd Styx" (*PL* II)—"abhorrèd rites to Hecate" (*Comus*): the ancient nether regions in both instances; "wingèd Warriour" (*PL* IV)—"wingèd Warriours" (*Circumcision*); "fringèd Bank" (*PL* IV)—"rushy-fringèd bank" (*Comus*); "helmèd head" (of the fallen angels—*PL* VI)— "helmèd Cherubim" (*Nat. Ode*). This relative abundance of close echoes would seem only natural if we agreed that Books I to VI of *PL* were the first substantial body of verse written by Milton since his early poems. Expressions from these poems, unobscured by much intermediate poetical composition, are likely in such a case still to have been alive in his mind. They would occur to him as he resumed the writing of verse. Sometimes they appeared with part of their context and sometimes not. They tended to reappear in their original form, so long as this was not incompatible with the style which Milton wished to adopt, i.e., in the above cases with the fully pronounced ending *-ed*. This impulse and these associations then wore off. This was especially likely to be the case if a prolonged break occurred in the process of composition—particularly if it were a break filled with harassing experiences, such as the collapse of the Commonwealth and the restoration of the Stuart monarchy, with the resulting danger to the poet. The old associations thereafter reappeared mainly as echoes from the latest verse composed by Milton, that is, the first half of *PL*, rather than from his early verse, the continuity of association with which was broken.

If any proof be needed of the tendency of the same expressions to appear in an unchanged form, though in varying contexts, in works that are more or less contiguous in time, a considerable amount of evidence can be produced from Milton's early poems, even if we confine ourselves to our list of *-ed* participles and participial adjectives: "charmèd wave" (*Nat. Ode*), "charmèd cup" and "charmèd band" (*Comus*); "abhorrèd rites" (*Comus*), "abhorrèd shears" (*Lycidas*); "removèd place" (*Il Penseroso*), "removèd climes" (in a cancelled passage from *Comus*); "ycie-pearlèd carr" (*Death of a Fair Infant*), "pearlèd wrists" (*Comus*); "pilèd Stones" (*On Shakespeare*), "pilèd Thunder" (*Vacation Exercise*).

The likelihood that, in addition to the natural process of the fading out of early associations, another factor already alluded to—namely, a change of stylistic attitude—caused Milton to use fewer forms in *-èd* in his late work, seems to be strengthened by the way he treats the expression *beloved.*[27] The usual pronunciation of the ending of this word in his time can hardly have been different from that of today. Nonetheless, this participial adjective, which does not occur until Book VI of *PL*, is used four times in the syncopated form "belov'd" (*PL* VI.680, X.70, *PR* I.85, IV.513) and only three times without the syncopation (*PL* X.489, *PR* I.32, 285).

It seems noteworthy how closely the results of the present examination correspond with those of our earlier analyses, particularly with those of our study of Milton's feminine endings.

VI

PYRRHIC VERSE ENDINGS

In the previous sections devices were discussed which after frequent occurrence in Milton's early poetry were used

27. How far this is a personal attitude of Milton's remains to be ascertained. There might be some connection between it and the fondness for the shorter forms, even where present-day usage prefers the longer ones, observable in late seventeenth- and eighteenth-century poets. Note, e.g., the scansions *learn'd* (Dryden, *Upon the Death of Lord Hastings* 71, *To My Honoured Kinsman, John Driden* 110; Pope, *Essay on Criticism* 92, 635, 740); *unlearn'd* (*Essay on Criticism* 327); *bless'd* (*To My Honoured Kinsman, John Driden* 1); *belov'd* (*Upon the Death of Lord Hastings* 94).

less and less or were entirely abandoned. But there are also instances of early devices which, while undergoing a late revival, are on closer examination found to have changed their artistic function. A case in point is the use in a terminal position of words of three or more syllables with only a slight secondary stress on the final syllable instead of the normal strong fifth beat, e.g., in *Comus*—"How charming is divine Philosophy!" (476), or in *SA*—"Then to love Bondage more than Liberty" (270). This final rhythm ("dactylic" or "pyrrhic"), which, if skillfully distributed, breaks the monotony of the terminal full stresses, is an early favorite of Milton's; however, it is used less frequently in *PL* I-VI, but occurs relatively often in *PL* VII-XII and becomes fairly prominent in *PR* and *SA*. At the same time the aesthetic implications of this rhythmical type change.

Our figures—absolute and, in parenthesis, in ratio per thousand lines—are as follows:

Comus: 101 (127.5).
PL (a): I—43 (53.9); II—32 (30.3); III—31 (41.8); IV—30 (29.6); V—29 (32.1); VI—17 (18.6). Total for Books I-VI: 182 (33.5).
PL (b): VII—26 (40.6); VIII—32 (49.3); IX—33 (27.8); X—51 (46.2); XI—33 (36.8); XII—23 (35.7). Total for Books VII-XII: 198 (38.6).
Total for *PL:* 380 (36.0).
PR: I—16 (31.9); II—38 (78.1); III—29 (65.5); IV—37 (57.9).
Total for *PR:* 120 (58.0).
SA: 69 (51.6).

The steep decline from *Comus* to *PL* I is followed by a further downward movement in *PL* I-VI, rather steady except for a relatively deep drop in *PL* III, but changing to a sudden ascent in *PL* VII. After this book the figures for the poem, while never quite reaching the level of *PL* I, keep well above the lowest level of *PL* I-VI. The average for the second half is perceptibly higher than that for the first half. *PR*, starting slightly below *PL* XII, then shows a steep rise in Book II, followed by a gradual decline leading it in Book IV rather close to the figure for *SA*. The averages both for *PR* and for *SA* considerably exceed that for the second half of *PL*. *PL* VII constitutes a boundary line, as we have seen it do on many earlier occasions, but the higher level which begins there never even approximately equals that of *Comus*, which represents an early extreme.

This is a familiar pattern which seems fully to agree with the chronological conclusions advanced in regard to both *PL* and *SA*.

The qualitative analysis of the rhythmical feature under consideration had best be preceded by a glance at the part it plays in earlier blank verse. Marlowe, who is the first author to use pyrrhic endings systematically, obviously relishes them. The 186 lines of the opening scene of *Tamburlaine* I have fifty-nine instances, seventeen of which are sonorous, exotic proper names (*Tamburlaine, Persepolis, Theridamas, Africa, Asia, India*, etc.) yielding an effect of thunderous stateliness. He also not infrequently uses final pyrrhics for lyrical purposes, e.g., in the opening speech of Act II, scene iii, of the Second Part:

> *The christall springs whose taste illuminates*
> *Refined eies with an eternal sight,*
> *Like tried siluer runs through Paradise*
> *To entertaine diuine* Zenocrate.
> *The Cherubins and holy Seraphins*
> *That sing and play before the king of kings,*
> *Vse all their voices and their instruments*
> *To entertaine diuine* Zenocrate.
> *And in this sweet and currious harmony,*
> *The God that tunes his musicke to our soules:*
> *Holds out his hand in highest maiesty*
> *To entertaine diuine* Zenocrate.

Even this brief excerpt should sufficiently convey the chanting effect of the passage, almost that of a sublime operatic aria. It also shows the stanzaic division effected by repeating a line that ends with a pyrrhic. Marlowe may have preferred this rhythm partly because it provided such a convenient means of using the imposing foreign polysyllables which he liked.[28] Shakespeare repeatedly produces similar stanzaic effects by means of terminal pyrrhics, but he does it more often than Marlowe by choosing less exotic expressions, e.g., in the speeches of Romeo and Juliet in Act III, Scenes ii and iii, of the tragedy, where the burdens used are the words "banishment" and "banishèd," or in Mark Antony's speech in *Julius Caesar* II.ii, where "ambitìous" appears as one of two refrain-like formulae. More frequently, this type of ending, occurring at more or less regular intervals, but without repetition of any one word,

---

28. See also, e.g., the refrains: "And ride in triumph through Persepolis" (1 *Tamburlaine* II.iv); "And shall I die, and this unconquered" (2 *Tamburlaine* V.iii); the refrain-like use of the name *Tamburlaine* (e.g., in 2 *Tamburlaine* III.v, IV.i, V.ii) or of the word *authority* (*Jew of Malta* V.128, 135, 138); and such rhyming and near-rhyming series as: *Syria, Egyptia, Africa, Scythia* (1 *Tamburlaine* I.ii); *pathetical, substantiàl* (*ibid.*); *perjury, purity, perjury, victory, perjury* (2 *Tamburlaine* II.ii); *majesty, Metropolis, Semiramis, victory, majesty, majesty, enemies* (*ibid.* II.v); *chivalry, magnanimity, majesty* (*ibid.* IV.i); *tyrannies, nobility, cruelty, majesty* (*ibid.*); *Persià, Arabià, Indià, Africa* (*ibid.* V.iii); *sovereignty, magnanimity, necessity, majesty, necessity, agony, Zenocrate, recovery, cruelty* (*ibid.*); *possessiòns, transgressiòn, professiòn* (*Jew of Malta* I.344, 348, 352); *righteousness, covetousness* (*ibid.* I.354, 356); *magnanimity, majesty, nobility* (*Edward II* 1322, 1324, 1325). In nearly all these instances, which could be multiplied, the above line-endings are so spaced as to subdivide the verse into stanza-like sections. Proper names and abstract nouns—especially such ending in -*y*—used in an emotional, "pathetical" fashion form the staple of this technique. Apart from examples with terminal vocalic (and often also consonantal) correspondences, which seem to accentuate the chanting lyrical nature of the verse, there are many without such echoes. Similar instances are not uncommon in the early Shakespeare. Cf., e.g., *deity, liberty, livery, monarchy* (*Rich. III*, I.i, 76, 77, 80, 83); *Lombardy, Italy, company* (*Taming of the Shrew* I.i.2, 4, 6); *Bentivolii, philosophy, philosophy, discipline* (*ibid.* I.i.13, 18, 28, 30); *harmony, prerogative, philosophy, harmony* (*ibid.* II.i.5, 6, 13, 14); *heraldry, maidenly, injury* (*Mids. N. D.* III.ii, 213, 217, 219).

forms a recurrent rhythmical motif helping to organize a passage, for instance, in Egeus' first accusatory speech in *A Midsummer Night's Dream* I.i, and in the opening speech of *Twelfth Night*—the former a set piece of well-proportioned rhetoric, the latter lyrical in tone. But there are also denser clusters of this type in Shakespeare, as well as many instances sprinkled with seeming irregularity over the pages.

Milton's practice in *Comus* seems closely to follow that of his Elizabethan predecessors. In the Elder Brother's speech on chastity, for example, which is a sort of aria on moral philosophy, a distinct quasi-stanzaic effect is produced by using the words *chastity* (4 times), *purity, majesty, virginity,* and *austerity* in final positions intermittently throughout the lyrical oration (418 ff.). These expressions—all strongly emotional abstract terms, related in meaning, and rhyming—clearly organize the rhythmical pattern of the passage. They do it with particular emphasis because most of them are placed before unmistakable final pauses. Together with other instances there are sixteen cases of such final pyrrhics in the fifty-seven lines of the speech—a ratio nearly as high as in the opening scene of *Tamburlaine*. A similar, if not quite so obvious, example of this technique is the Lady's highly eloquent speech on the same theme in lines 756-799, where this device is found thirteen times in forty-four lines. The tone of lyrical oratory remains very pronounced, but the quasi-stanzaic subdivision is blurred by the more frequent lack of distinct terminal pauses. Most of the expressions used for the verse endings are again abstract terms with emotional overtones quite as strong as in the former speech, and even the rhymes reappear, though not so abundantly: *Temperance, Luxury, gluttony, ingratitude, mystery, Virginity, Rhetorick, vehemence.* This is a lyrical and rhetorical technique closely akin to that of Marlowe and Shakespeare. Another feature of *Comus* reminding one more specifically of Marlowe is the relatively frequent appearance

of romantic or exotic proper names or other exotically fla-
vored expressions with pyrrhic endings in terminal positions: *Naiades, Arcady, Hecate, Acheron, Helena, Erebus,
Guendolen, Asphodel.*[29] The archaic pronunciations *visiòn,
suspiciòn, contagiòn, Consciènce, apparitiòn, self-delusiòn,
Contemplatiòn, conditiòn, complexiòn,*[30] resorted to in order
to obtain this rhythmical effect, are also thoroughly Elizabethan. Milton here seems to use final pyrrhics for "melliflu-
ous" lyrical and sonorous oratorical effects; their function of
subdividing a passage in near-stanzaic fashion also resembles
the technique of lyrical poetry.

In *PL* the examples, while generally few and far between,
occasionally appear in clusters suggesting special artistic
purposes which seem capable of rough classification.

A. *Romantic and exotic effects.* These occur in only two
well-marked "clusters," in *PL* I.582-585 and *PL* II.552-565.
In the former, a momentary brilliant resuscitation of "Fable
or Romance," splendid dactylic proper names supply the atmosphere: "And all who since, Baptiz'd or Infidel / Jousted
in *Aspramont* or *Montalban,* / *Damasco,* or *Marocco,* or
Trebisond." In the latter the mood is more gentle and melancholy, and abstract terms charged with feeling, all of
which also appear in *Comus* in the same metrical position
(*harmony, ravishment, misery, Philosophy*), serve to echo
the effect produced by "notes Angelical" on the fallen spirits.
The situation closely resembles that of Comus—likewise an
evil spirit rapturously sensitive to music—listening to the
Lady's song. The similarity of the subject is reflected in the
rhythmical method, and even in the actual wording, for these
lines are full of reminiscences from the passage in *Comus*
alluded to, as well as from other parts of the masque.[31]

29. *Comus* 254, 340, 535, 604, 676, 804, 831, 842.
30. *Comus* 298, 412, 467, 212, 641, 365, 377, 685, 749.
31. Compare the following parallels: "to all Heav'ns Harmonies" (*Comus*
243)—"But the harmony" (*PL* II.552); "such divine inchanting ravishment"

No other passages containing clusters of final pyrrhics combine romance and lyricism in a comparable manner. Their stylistic flavor in the later books is different. True, the same rhythm is rather marked in the exordium to Book IX, where Milton again deals with the romance of chivalry, but this time in a tone suggesting caustic sarcasm. The rhythm —five instances of our type within fifteen lines—may have occurred to him together with the subject matter. The emphasis here, however, is certainly not on the romance but on the antiromantic philosophy: this is austere rhetoric, not lyricism. But the rhetoric is not unemotional, and it is aptly reinforced by the rhythm. This leads us to our second category.

B. *Religious or ethical lyricism and oratory.* The hymn of the angels to the Almighty in *PL* III.372 ff. has five final pyrrhics in fourteen lines (372-385), most of them in abstract words suggestive of lofty emotion: *Omnipotent, Infinite, invisible, Seraphim, Divine Similitude.* Only three of these come in strictly end-stopped lines, but their effect is to introduce definite rhythmical grouping into the first part of the long hymn before it falls back on other rhythmical methods.

In the description of the "Chariot of Paternal Deitie" in VI.749 ff. an approximation of a stanzaic effect is achieved by the terminal use, at due intervals, of words with majestic reverberations: *Deitie, Firmament, Victorie*—three cases in thirteen lines.

After this passage the lyrical use of pyrrhic endings in *PL* appears to cease, unless one sees traces of it in VIII.360-366, 381-392, and 419-431, where we also find some near-

---

(*Comus* 245)—"took with ravishment / The thronging audience" (*PL* II.554) (with which should also be compared "Who as they sung, would take the prison'd soul, / And lap it in *Elysium*" [*Comus* 256, 257]); "She that has that, is clad in compleat steel" (*Comus* 421)—"With stubborn patience as with triple steel" (*PL* II.569); "How charming is divine Philosophy" (*Comus* 476)—"Vain wisdom all, and false Philosophy" (*PL* II.565).

stanzaic subdivision.[32] The emotional quality is even more conspicuous by its absence in the purely abstract, technical, or neutral instances, clusters of which are found in Raphael's account of the physical constitution of angelic beings (*PL* V.410-416), in the description of Adam's repast with the angel (*ibid.* 424-449), in the episode concerning the punishment of Satan and his associates (X.541-554), and in the grave, objective narrative in *PL* XI.661-675. The old rhythms reappear, but with little of the characteristic earlier manner. Two passages, in *PL* III.475-480 and *PL* XI.480-487, the former in the episode about the Paradise of Fools, the latter in the catalogue of diseases in the lazar house scene, use terminal pyrrhics with considerable realistic force but without any lyrical quality. This exhausts my list of clusters of this type of ending in *PL*.

There appears a definite trend in this pattern of development. Used rather copiously in *Comus* as a strongly emotional rhetorico-lyrical device derived from the Elizabethans, this rhythmical type becomes much rarer in *PL;* but where clusters of it occur in the earlier books they tend to retain something of the manner and the associations of Milton's early verse. In the later books the emotional use of pyrrhic line endings appears even more seldom, and then only in

32. These three passages—containing clusters of three, five, and five instances each—all occur in Adam's speeches to the Deity when he urgently appeals to God for a companion; significantly, the same rhythm does not appear even once in the calm replies of the Lord. Adam's language, though abstract and somewhat didactic, is colored with emotion: it is logical argument suffused with feeling. The words used are partly too intellectual or technical, in Milton's late manner, to admit of much lyricism, but others are of a philosophico-emotional or a more purely lyrical type: *Universe, liberal, solitude; substitute, societie, disparitie, participate, Lioness; infinite, manifest, multiplied, amitie, deified.* They are placed at intervals, often so short as to divide the verse into couplets, but sufficiently regular to produce definite rhythmical grouping, which, however, is slightly obscured by run-on effects. The lyrical tendency is weakened and seems only faintly to echo the *Comus* manner.

a considerably weakened form. The last case of obvious quasi-stanzaic grouping is in Book VIII.

One of the leading themes of *PR* is the systematic contrasting of temperance and self-control with the temptations of self-indulgent luxury and worldly glory. Into his descriptions of mundane magnificence Milton has concentrated much of his earlier brilliant coloring, reverting to many of his old stylistic and rhythmical methods, including terminal pyrrhics, which occur not infrequently in exotic, richly suggestive proper names and their equivalents. While the poet's philosophy condemns the things he depicts, he nevertheless depicts them in much the old manner. We have accordingly several examples of category A, but usually in a brief, condensed form, and consequently without any stanzaic effect: (1) in Satan's contemptuous reference to Belial's excessively philogynic proclivities (II.186-187: *Clymene, Antiopa*); (2) in the highly-colored description of the sybaritic banquet to which Satan invites Christ (II.355-361: *Naiades, Lyones, Pellenore*); (3) in a romantic simile inserted into a picture of martial splendor (III.341-344: *Angelica, Charlemane, Chivalrie*). A panorama of worldly grandeur on an even larger scale is presented in IV.34-75, where the same type reappears throughout a rather long passage, on this occasion producing in places some recognizable rhythmical subdivision: *elevate, Aqueducts, Cittadel, Palatine, Architects, Artificers, Provinces, Chersoness, Taprobane*. These expressions, with their familiar cadence and magnificent associations, evoke the old atmosphere for the last time: henceforward Milton has done with worldly luxury, which even here he portrays only to condemn.

Type B occurs only in a considerably intellectualized form, with little lyrical fervor even in the final hymn of the angels in Book IV, where the old rhythms nevertheless revive for a moment: *vanquishing, Paradise, fraudulent* (607-610). The remaining instances appear in II.407-423, where Satan, drawing on all his rhetorical resources, tries to persuade Christ of the need for wealth as a means to glory, using this rhythmical effect, among others, to organize his carefully built-up address *(appetite, enterprise, Multitude, Edomite)*; in III.82-89, where Christ, with subdued urgency, discusses the merits and demerits of ancient philosophy *(Sacrifice, violence, eminent, Conquerours)*; and in the same book, 410-420, where the degradation of Israel is exposed by him with quiet but strong rhetoric *(Israelites, Deities, Ashtaroth, captivity)*.

The two remaining clusters (*PR* I.154-160, II.78-81) are even more quiet and quite unemphatic. In *PR* as a whole the spontaneous lyrical feeling associated with final pyrrhics has disappeared altogether: a deliberately staged revival of its emotional use is found only in passages recreating the former atmosphere in order to deprecate it. Elsewhere there are still some indications of a mildly rhetorical use of the device.

As for *SA*, clusters of such endings have become very rare and are never dense in the nonlyrical dialogue. It may be because of the calculated oratory of Dalila that we find them more often in her speeches than anywhere else: *counterpois'd, infirmity, mutable, liberty, Philistines* (770-808); and *Circumcis'd, famousest, festivals, Ephraim, piety* (975-996). The slow stateliness of the speech reporting Samson's death may have been purposely enhanced by the verse endings: *spectacle, Theatre, Sacrifice, immediately, Antagonist*. But there is only faint quasi-stanzaic grouping; the effect of these passages is sober and carries no suggestion of Milton's youthful manner.

A considerable part is played by this device in the odes and lyrical monologues of the tragedy, but the austere dignity of the effects has none of the semioperatic aria atmosphere of *Tamburlaine* and parts of *Comus*. Read, for instance:

> *He would not else* ...
> *Have prompted this Heroic* Nazarite,
> *Against his vow of strictest purity,*
> *To seek in marriage that fallacious Bride,*
> *Unclean, unchaste.*
>
> (315-320)

Or again:

> *He led me on to mightiest deeds*
> *Above the nerve of mortal arm*
> *Against the uncircumcis'd, our enemies,*
> *But now hath cast me off as never known,*
> *And to those cruel enemies....*
>
> (638-641)

The role of the pyrrhic endings in forming the complex rhythmical patterns of the lyrical parts of the tragedy can hardly be analyzed without far exceeding the limits of this paper.

It should seem clear from the above examination that, aesthetically speaking, the nature of Milton's terminal use of pyrrhics in *SA* stands at the opposite pole from *Comus:* it makes us think of the ancient prophets, of Aeschylus or Sophocles, rather than of the music of pastoral or of the seductions of the romance of chivalry.

This, it might be objected, is due to the obvious difference between biblical tragedy and pastoral. Such an objection might indeed stand, had we not been able to observe closely the gradual change of the aesthetic atmosphere characteristic of passages with pyrrhic line endings in Milton. The progress from lyrical fervor to austerity of tone could be traced step by step throughout *PL*, leading us farther and farther away from *Comus* and nearer and nearer to *SA*. It is this steady continuity of change that is remarkable and

supports the traditional Miltonic chronology, in close agreement with our findings in the earlier sections of this essay.

VII

CONCLUSION

Glancing back over the entire field covered in the preceding analyses, I find it difficult to avoid the conclusion
that there can hardly be anything very wrong with the
traditional chronology of Milton's major poems or their parts.
The continuity in the statistical sequences is too striking,
and the emerging patterns occur too persistently and seem
too natural to be accidental. Certain features in particular,
such as the treatment of feminine endings, of syllabized -*ed*
endings, and of terminal pyrrhics, show a compelling logic
in their development with which no order of composition
very different from the traditionally accepted one seems at
all compatible. The frequency with which major changes
in trends of development begin in the middle of *PL*, especially in Book VII, agrees remarkably with Professor J. H.
Hanford's view that the composition of the poem was probably interrupted midway by the fall of the Commonwealth;
especially the handling of -*ed* endings lends strong support
to the theory that Book VII was the first part of the epic to
be composed after the Restoration. The second half of *PL*
is linked in so many ways with *PR*, and *PR*, in its turn, with
SA, that the chronological sequence *PL* VII-XII: *PR*: *SA*
seems inescapable.

This does not mean that smaller portions of these works
may not have been composed somewhat out of sequence.
However, in spite of a good deal of statistical experimentation, I have failed to discover any convincing evidence of
such chronological dislocation. There may, indeed, seem to
be some difficulties with Books III and XI of *PL*, which more

often than any others present special features differentiating them from their environment.

Such features with regard to Book III are: (1) an unusually low proportion of medial strong pauses; (2) a scarcity of run-on lines, and (3) a scarcity of strong pauses in the first half of the line. All these peculiarities suggest less than the normal amount of metrical experimentation. Points (1) and (2) are characteristic manifestations of a leaning towards an end-stopped technique. The resulting effect of regularity, of a diminution of that tension between the syntactic and the metrical structure which is so prominent in the beginning of *PL*, agrees with the relatively undramatic nature of Book III, which seems quite deliberately contrasted with the turbulency of the first two books. On closer examination, we find that especially the narrative, which in this book is much more slow and measured than in the first two books, abounds in long sequences of lines without any strong internal pauses. But even the speeches, despite their somewhat greater dramatic intensity, have comparatively few strong pauses within lines. The calm dignity of the Father and Son seems to be strongly emphasized in purposeful contrast to the restless passion of the infernal spirits in the previous books, with its more staccato rhythms. The special prosody of this book appears, then, to have been deliberately intended or instinctively adopted to produce a specific effect to fit the very distinctive part which this book plays in the poem. At this highly important turning point the need for a sharp differentiation from the preceding books was so exceptionally strong that it resulted in the adoption of an unusual rhythmical pattern. It seems consequently unnecessary to assume the existence of any chronological puzzle.

Book XI is more difficult. Its special features are: (1) a conspicuously high frequency of all strong pauses (with the terminal and medial pauses fairly well balanced); (2)

a low proportion of polysyllables near the beginning of the line; (3) a scarcity of feminine endings and a total absence of unvoiced consonants in such endings; (4) the presence of independent -*ed* links with the early poems in the story of the Deluge. In addition, Book XI shares with Book X the peculiarity of (5) a rather low proportion of strong pauses occurring after an unstressed syllable. Points (3), (4), and (5) seem to link Book XI with the first half of *PL*. Some of these anomalies, however, are directly due to the unusual prosody of one single passage, the section dealing with the Deluge, which is conspicuous not only for its -*ed* links with the early period, but also (in XI.708-783) for its exceptional number of strong medial pauses, especially in the first half of the line—characteristic features of *PL* I-IV—which noticeably heighten the total frequency of strong pauses in the book. These features may possibly lend some countenance to Professor A. H. Gilbert's theory that this is relatively early work. But while the presence of some such early matter is by no means impossible, the neatness with which Book XI—especially without this one passage—fits into a number of other statistical sequences, e.g., those for run-on lines, for middle and extreme strong pauses, and for polysyllables near the end of the line, suggests that on the whole it occupies its right chronological place.[33]

33. This becomes even more obvious if we treat *PL* XI and XII as one book, as Milton himself did in the first edition of his epic. He seems often to have worked by means of balanced rhythmical contrasts which, viewed statistically, cancel each other out. Such contrasts are especially frequent between contiguous books. The ups and downs in such books are in many cases almost exactly equal. Represented graphically, as in sections I and II of the present paper, these differences often result in zigzag lines of considerable regularity. If, instead of being treated individually, the different books of *PL* had been considered in groups of two, the resulting figures would frequently have had to be represented by almost straight lines. I give a few examples:
    (a) Run-on lines: *PL* I-II, 65.3%; III-IV, 57.8%; V-VI, 59.9%; VII-VIII, 56.3%; IX-X, 56.0%; XI-XII, 56.8%.

As was emphasized at the beginning of this paper, any conclusions here reached can be considered valid only for Milton's text as it stands. Even though earlier drafts may be embedded in the final versions, the thoroughness with which the poet would appear to have recast such drafts makes it improbable, save in some exceptional cases, that they could be recognized by any anachronistic peculiarities of their prosody: they are likely in most cases to have been so completely remolded even in their rhythmical texture that they no longer stand out. As for the text in its final form, it would

---

(b) Strong pauses in the first half of lines: *PL* I-II, 39.2%; III-IV, 42.3%; V-VI, 41.6%; VII-VIII, 44.1%; IX-X, 38.5%; XI-XII, 33.7%.

(c) Strong pauses in the second half of lines: *PL* I-II, 42.8%; III-IV, 42.3%; V-VI, 45.6%; VII-VIII, 45.9%; IX-X, 48.9%; XI-XII, 52.5%.

(d) Feminine pauses: *PL* I-II, 33.9%; III-IV, 25.6%; V-VI, 31.0%; VII-VIII, 32.2%; IX-X, 33.6%; XI-X, 31.6%.

(e) Initial and near-initial polysyllables: *PL* I-II, 41.1%; III-IV, 41.2%; V-VI, 42.6%; VII-VIII, 33.1%; IX-X, 41.2%; XI-XII, 35.6%.

Sharp contrasts have become very scarce in these figures. Long successions of percentages show only minute divergences, e.g., *PL* VII-XII in (a), *PL* III-VIII in (b), *PL* V-XII in (d), *PL* I-VI in (e). In (c) the figures fall into three groups of four books each, ascending terrace fashion. In (b) the descent through *PL* VII-XII is quite straight. Zigzag lines, if regular, look straight when viewed from a sufficient distance.

In the above sequences both *PL* III and *PL* XI have in most cases been neatly absorbed into the total patterns, since *PL* IV and *PL* XII supplement their numerical deficits and smooth out their surpluses. The rhythmical waves of which Books III and XI form parts do not protrude in the total design. Because of its regularity, the undulation observed in many of the graphs of sections I and II subsides to a surprising extent as soon as the successive books of *PL* are grouped in pairs. This complementary distribution of opposed rhythmical movements in consecutive books occurs somewhat too frequently to be attributed to mere coincidence. It seems to suggest a close proximity in time between the books thus linked. It likewise indicates a keen sense of large-scale symmetry in Milton's treatment of rhythm.

One of the numerous readers of this paper before its appearance in print suggests that some of the metrical peculiarities of *PL* XI, e.g., its scarcity of feminine endings, may be due to its being largely narrative. My figures for the narrative and the dramatic parts, however, do not warrant this conclusion. See note 17. I have been unable to discover anything approaching a consistent metrical differentiation of the speeches from the narrative passages of *PL*. There are contrasts, but their nature varies.

seem that the traditional chronology, in its salient features, is difficult to assail. All theories intended to revolutionize it rely on highly circumstantial and conjectural evidence and have subjective elements in them, as Professor W. R. Parker for his part frankly concedes. The evidence here presented is not complete—a legion of scholars would be needed to make it such—but it covers a considerable variety of important and characteristic features and rests on an objective basis. Perhaps it may be of sufficient weight to justify adhering to the conventional chronology of Milton's blank verse poems.

APPENDIX

PROSODICAL DEVELOPMENT IN *SAMSON AGONISTES*

In the following tables *SA* has been subdivided into three parts. *A* includes the pentameters of the first two actlike sections, lines 1-276 and 331-605; *B*, those of the next two, 721-1009 and 1061-1267; and *C*, those in the final section, 1307-1744. The resulting amounts of blank verse—474, 492, and 372 lines respectively—are sufficient for our statistical purposes, whereas the first four "acts," taken individually, would have been too short. The divisions—Samson in dejection, Samson roused to indignation, and Samson preparing for, and then performing, his final heroic feat—correspond to the main movements of the drama.

STRONG PAUSES

	Total	Terminal	Medial	First half	Exact middle	Second half	Extreme pauses	Feminine pauses	Lines without terminal punctuation	Feminine endings	Final pyrrhics
A.	190	108	82	26	10	46	32	31	210	54	21
B.	182	137	45	17	6	22	13	19	212	102	27
C.	176	136	40	18	6	16	13	13	141	86	21

POLYSYLLABLES

	Initial and near-initial	Middle	Terminal and near-terminal	Total	Number of lines
A.	17	18	8	43	474
B.	14	19	15	48	492
C.	9	18	18	45	372

These figures, translated into ratios, yield the following results:

STRONG PAUSES

	Total (per 1000 lines)	Terminal (per 1000 lines)	Medial (per 1000 lines)	Term.:Med.	First half	Exact middle	Second half	Extreme pauses	Feminine pauses	Lines without terminal punctuation	Feminine endings (per 1000 lines)	Final pyrrhics (per 1000 lines)
A.	400	227	173	57%:43%	32%	12%	56%	39%	38%	44%	114	44
B.	370	279	91	75%:25%	38%	13%	49%	42%	42%	43%	207	55
C.	473	366	107	77%:23%	45%	15%	40%	32%	32%	38%	231	57

POLYSYLLABLES

	Total (per 1000 lines)	Initial and near-initial	Middle	Terminal and near-terminal
A.	91	39%	42%	19%
B.	97	29%	40%	31%
C.	121	20%	40%	40%

Steady progression or regression is the most striking characteristic of the majority of these ratios: of those for pauses in the first half, the middle, and the second half of the line; for terminal and medial pauses in relation to each other; for lines without any final punctuation; for feminine and pyrrhic endings; and for polysyllables. Sometimes *B* is closer to *A* than to *C*, and sometimes vice versa. In some instances, as in the case of pauses in the first and the second half of pentameters, or of polysyllables near the beginning or the end of the line, *B* is almost equidistant from both *A* and *C*. This steadiness of direction suggests a subconscious unity of impulse and inspiration that could hardly have survived such prolonged interruptions of the process of composition as Professor W. R. Parker thinks probable. It seems likelier that *SA* was composed rapidly—at the rate of twenty lines a day it could have been done in three months—which might explain the occasional lack of meticulous finish, or even the ruggedness, in its style that Professor A. H. Gilbert has noticed. In contrast to *PR* with its elaborate polish, which apparently took years to achieve, *SA* appears to owe its existence to a powerful emotional impulse, which may well have speeded up its production. It seems the final mighty spurt of an athlete of the spirit, performed with incomparable virtuosity, but, in places, also with some Aeschylean neglect of those minor graces that must have seemed more essential for *PR* than for a tragedy of Michelangelesque power.